A Year of Nothing New

TOOLS FOR LIVING LEAN AND GREEN

Kristin Skarie

A Year of Nothing New – Tools for Living Lean and Green
Copyright © 2013 by Nothing New

Published by Nothing New
2604 Elmwood Avenue, #246
Rochester, NY 14618
www.betterteams.com
585.330.9181

This book was printed on paper containing 100% post-consumer recycled fiber.

Cover art by Monica Guilian
Edited by Dan Seseske
Layout by Josh Visser
Back Cover Photo by Ryan T. Collier Photography LLC
Printed by Color House Graphics, Grand Rapids, MI

The Library of Congress has cataloged this edition as follows:
    "A year of nothing new"
    2013916013

Nothing New Publishing

    A Year of Nothing New – Tools for Living Lean and Green
    ISBN 978-0-9890298-0-3

Printed in the United States of America

·FIRST EDITION

13 14 15 16 // 5 4 3 2 1

"If everyone would do one thing they have the time and energy to do...no matter how small or inconsequential they think it might be...it would make all the difference."

– Susan B. Anthony, Activist/suffragist (1820-1906)

12·5·13

Brian—
For all you do
to green your corner
of the world — Thank you!
And for your kindnesses as
a colleague and friend :)

Have a Nothing
New Day!
~peace,
Kristi

Dedication

To YOU – who are doing your part in taking care of our Earth and its inhabitants to multiply your positive impact, reduce your footprint and focus on what really matters.

Contents

Introduction
THE BACK STORY

"Imagine no possessions, I wonder if you can."

– John Lennon,
Singer/songwriter (1940-1980)

What do you want? What do you need? What can't you live without? Take a moment...visualize how great you would look wearing those new shoes you just saw in the catalog. Picture how connected you would be talking on the latest phone everyone seems to have...how happy you would be with the new sheets and comforter (with matching pillows) on your bed, how your friends would rave about your new curtains and your family would be impressed by the new dishes on the table for your holiday dinner. Envision how satisfied you would be with that new car, computer, television, bike, picture frame, lamp, dress, espresso maker, house, purse, necklace, basketball, fishing rod or bestselling book. Now think about delaying all of these and other new purchases for one year. Hard to imagine and even harder to do?

The concept of putting off any new purchases for 365 days was not in my plans at all. I enjoyed shopping as a skill set, an activity, even as entertainment ("Let's go shopping!"). I enjoyed buying new clothes, presents for others (and myself), and things for my house, yard and garden. I have always been privileged to be fairly unrestricted with my purchasing power. OK, stop, rephrase – I was VERY

FREE to purchase most anything I wanted, within reason of course – I am not talking yachts, planes or football teams. This "disposable income" (as in discard, throw away, scrap, ditch and jettison) was certainly being disposed of on a regular basis. I was able to meet most of my personal and business financial obligations so it seemed there was no urgent need to radically change my spending behavior.

However, I knew in the back of my mind I was not always making the best choices. I was allowing myself to succumb to holiday shopping, not trying hard enough to look for the best prices and giving in too easily to the pull of special sales and seasonal promotions. The use of credit was stretching my financial security quite thin and I was definitely not donating as much as I would have liked to my causes. There were some other money issues to address and although I was working on them, I always had a nagging feeling about not having saved enough for emergencies or retirement. My buyer's remorse was starting to become uncomfortable. The new things I was buying did not seem to last very long – it felt like the buying was producing short-lived joy and lacked the sustainability I desired. These same feelings were showing up in other areas and had me questioning how I was managing my work life and navigating my personal life. There was a disturbance in the force.

Then I met Terri Scanlon of *Reslife.net* at a conference in Boston on March 19, 2010. This fantastic woman shared her story at a pre-conference dinner about a year of not buying anything new. I was intrigued. Her husband had read an article in the New York Times about a family who spent a year "not shopping". When he casually shared the idea with Terri as a conversation point, he never dreamed her response would be "OK!" "What do you mean OK?" was his counter-response! Thus launched their discussion of what a year of conscious consumption would look like for them. They embarked on a year of learning – choosing to spend, eat and live very differently. They de-cluttered, scaled back, streamlined and ultimately freed themselves from material things. The deliberation to examine their expenditures, reduce their impact on the earth and live with less was compelling.

"Exactly what I need", I thought as I applied the new lip gloss purchased minutes before. I am always up for a challenge and bought in immediately. I decided to follow Terri's path to greener living and began a "Nothing New" journey of my own. I made a mindful decision that day to delay all new purchases for one year and pay attention to the spending ripple effect of what I buy, use and throw away.

A spontaneous decision, it seemed easy and obvious at the time. I was becoming really frustrated with how many things we buy are not made in the USA (clothing, shoes, house items, furniture... everything?). I had always been annoyed by how easily things break but was becoming increasingly perturbed by how much more often I was buying new instead of used and choosing store-bought over home-made. This seemed perfect – for values realignment and simplification.

I was not sure at the time, what this commitment would mean, how it would play out or the impact it would have on how I view my life. I didn't know then how the year would evolve into endless possibilities. During the year, I explored all aspects of how I was spending (and wasting) my resources – money, time, and energy – and looked deeply at how my life affects others. A range of personal and work decision-making opportunities unfolded, from tiny alterations of daily tasks and projects to more complex ending of commitments and shifting relationships.

The long-term focus on conscious consumption, instead of random shopping, gave me a lot of time to think about the "why" of all of this. This was the number two question after, "What about food?" My why became clear and easy to explain...Turns out I had been greening my life all along and the roots of my reduce-reuse-recycle philosophy ran deep. They resurfaced as I was addressing the mess from a recent move aka "going through way too many boxes in the garage I had not looked in for years." The de-cluttering process was a joyous secondary outcome of my Nothing New year. In the cleaning, I found my Girl Scout sash from 4th grade causing me to backtrack mentally through my scouting days. I remembered the "Action 70s" pin given to us as a motivator for service and pluralism. At the time, I wondered what would happen after the 70s were over. Would the action subside? Would we somehow be done? Would there be a new pin for the "Action 80s"? I was of course blissfully unaware of the pending puffy hair, shoulder pads and leg warmers – I have photos. Or would we (would I?) keep caring for more elderly folks, recycling more bottles, organizing more can drives, building stronger communities, reading to more children and cleaning up more roadways? The answer was yes...and we're still not done! I always recycled, camped responsibly and volunteered when I could. However, I had not done anything dramatic to really change the way I spent (my money, time and energy), ate, shopped and worked. This make, do, or do without year turned into a "capstone project" taking my personal Action 70s to a new level!

Looking back on the year, many new habits were very difficult to initiate and were therefore more rewarding when put into place. Some parts of the year were easy and the resulting new behaviors turned into sustainable habits. Best of all, people shared their stories with me about what they do to live more deliberately, minimize their impact on the earth and serve others in simple yet profound ways. There was inspiration at every junction. I turned my wants, needs and haves inside out, laundered them, and hung them to dry to look at every angle of my spending.

The Rolling Stones lyrics became a bit of a mantra, "Oh you can't always get what you want/but if you try sometimes/you just might find/you get what you need". Indeed. In addition to the beginning of a personal financial turnaround with the money saved from Nothing New, I had a health, fitness, nutrition and service renaissance. Freed from shopping and the desire for new stuff, I released myself from activities (and a few relationships) inconsistent with how I wanted to spend my time...I bought time! Time to volunteer, garden, swim, read, and write. I became serendipitously involved as a Pencil Partner for the Rochester City School District and am now in the process of reviving the creation of my not-for-profit organiza- tion called "Plant a Seed, Make a Difference" to improve educational, environmental and economic health for people and their commu- nities. Most significantly, I am building a financial reserve to help friends and family in times of need and to contribute to my favorite charities.

As for the Girl Scouts, I am forever beholden for the abundant lessons – the appreciation and care for the outdoors, the confidence to live on my own and the value of community and connection. The now-vintage sash pin unearthed from a long unopened, post-move storage bin reminds me we are never really done with serving others, caring for the earth, and being thoughtful in our use of resources. Not only about money, my Year of Nothing New offered lessons about spending my time and energy in deliberate ways. It helped me let go of an overload of commitments to leave room for the right responsibilities. It was like one long Girl Scout work weekend! Instead of cleaning cabins, fixing latrines and clearing trails, I got to use an intense, extended time period to focus on my priorities and to be more true to my values. I have a revived responsibility for what I purchase, use, waste and throw away and a renewed assurance that I can live on so much less and with so much less.

The Girl Scout Laws – 1912

1. A Girl Scout's Honor is to be Trusted

2. A Girl Scout Is Loyal

3. A Girl Scout's Duty Is to be Useful and to Help Others

4. A Girl Scout is a Friend to All, and a Sister to every other Girl Scout no matter to what Social Class she May Belong

5. A Girl Scout Is Courteous

6. A Girl Scout Keeps Herself Pure

7. A Girl Scout Is a Friend to Animals

8. A Girl Scout Obeys Orders

9. A Girl Scout is Cheerful

10. A Girl Scout is Thrifty

The Girl Scout Law – 2013

I will do my best to be honest and fair, friendly and helpful, considerate and caring, courageous and strong, and responsible for what I say and do, and to respect myself and others, respect authority, use resources wisely, make the world a better place, and be a sister to every Girl Scout.

My faith is restored in the impact one person can have on her own life, the people around her and on the earth. Let me show you how you can green your living to change the way you consume and the way you spend to make a bigger, better more sustainable life with less. Have a Nothing New Day!

PONDER THIS...

- When have you had a defining/milestone event that shifted your thinking, your learning, or your relationships?

- What habits from your younger days have carried over to your life now?

- What would you do differently if you had "more time in the day?"

- How does the way you spend your money, your time and your energy reflect the life you want to lead?

- Who do you refer to or consult with when making decisions on how you spend your energy, your time and/or your money?

Privilege
POWER TO PURCHASE

"Live simply, so that all may simply live."

– Elizabeth Ann Seton,
Founder of Saint Joseph's Academy and Free School (1774-1821)

In college, I had a pin on my wallet with the above quotation to prompt me to be careful with my money. It served as a beacon to be fully aware of the financial choices I was making. I wanted to be constantly reminded of the privilege I had of having spending money. I was able to earn enough money at my summer lifeguarding job to pay for tuition (those days are long gone). Eventually, I had an on-campus job as a House Fellow (Resident Assistant), which allowed me to come out of college with minimal debt (a thing of the past for most of today's college graduates).

By virtue of me starting this section with, "In college, I...", means I am in a position of privilege and part of a small group of people who have been to college. A Huffington Post story offers this; According to a new study out of Harvard University, 6.7% of the world's population has a college degree. Let's do the math – with over 7 billion people in the world, 6.7% is 47 million people, or the population equivalent of Spain. Compared to the other 653 million people on earth who do not have a college degree it is surely a privilege to have had this opportunity.

In addition to going to college, I graduated with a Bachelor's degree – it's a wonder really, when I think of the last minute papers, mind-numbing science courses and the F on my transcript for the 7:45am ballet class. Coupled with going on for a Master's degree, education was and is a factor of privilege in almost every aspect of my life.

Privilege is defined by Merriam-Webster as "a right or immunity granted as a peculiar benefit, advantage, or favor." I was granted the "right" to go to college because of the financial access, emotional support and intellectual preparation in place for me. The US Census Bureau has recently reported that a college degree can nearly double a person's annual income. My college education – a permanent credential – gives me more earning power and many other benefits. I have advantages in other areas of my life – who I am and what has been given to me. I have entrée to almost any job, restaurant, doorway, airplane, or highway I desire. Except for my age I suppose. Since I am now (way) over 25, some would say I am in the "older person" category and at a disadvantage for certain jobs. Maybe true, except there are things I know and am able to do because of my age, not in spite of it.

Much opportunity has been afforded to me. I grew up in a suburb of a large city, lived in a safe neighborhood, walked to school, and went to day camp. Along with Girl Scouts, I participated in team sports and had viable part-time jobs. My parents went to college, we knew most of our neighbors (my mom is still living in the house I grew up in) and there was a public outdoor pool a 5 minute walk from home. At the risk of sounding like I am bragging, I tell you these things in order for you to know I KNOW how blessed I am to make a decision to live greener and do without as a temporary experiment. Many people never buy anything new or have NOTHING. Many people in my town and yours do not have their basic food, clothing and shelter needs met. I am able to make decisions about how I use my income and spend my money on things beyond the basics.

Many other success factors played a role in me being able to do what I do now. I can read. I have health insurance, time and space to grow a garden, access to credit, and drive a working car. I feel safe in my house, contribute regularly to a retirement account and have two cats. I own a home with room for a pony (British comedy *Keeping Up Appearances* reference – hee hee) and can afford to travel for pleasure. I affirm I am in need of nothing. I have been given many blessings from Jesus that do not show up as success factors as far as research reports are concerned. Oh, and I am super funny – which is clearly an advantage.

Being highly aware of what I HAVE was one of the most compelling, early, in-my-face, reminders as I launched my Year of Nothing New. Understanding my "haves" helped me better discern between my "wants" and "needs"...I wish you the same! It is a spring-cleaning venture to realign, reinvest, relearn and perhaps rediscover what's really important to you.

PONDER THIS...

- What do you have or have access to giving you advantages in your life?

- What success factors were in place for you growing up?

- What success factors are you aware of on a daily basis giving you privilege?

- What privilege areas are you least aware of on a daily basis?

- How do you differentiate between what you need and what you want?

- What do you need? What do you want?

The Year

SETTING UP THE CHALLENGE

"There are years that ask questions and years that answer."

– Zora Neale Hurston,
Folklorist/author (1891-1960)

In the midst of a particularly challenging 2009, my cousin in-law Carrie Leutenegger sent me a beautiful, supportive card with the above quote – now framed and placed on the dresser in my bedroom for daily viewing. I was sure the card was a predictor of all of the answers I would unearth in a hopeful 2010. I would look back with a knowing nod, squinty eyes and say, "Oh now I understand everything," in a wise and deliberate tone. Not quite. I gathered more questions with limited answers and learned more from tilling the problems than in sowing the solutions. Over and over, "…you might find you get what you need…" kept presenting itself in various projects, friendships and commitments. Looking back, the unrest in 2009 had me primed for a new way of living and being open to entertain the awaiting Nothing New Challenge.

My initial Nothing New "why" was merely a "why not?" – the excitement of trying something new. I didn't think anyone would be particularly interested in the experiment and was happy to be doing this for myself. I thought it would be a refreshing change and perhaps a necessary shift in my life. It was. Once into the year, friends and colleagues encouraged me to blog about the year (thank you Art Goldin), which I had never done before. I started in July and was grateful to reflect on what I learned from the blogging process and my followers!

The emerging reasons were more compelling – I began to track, measure and quantify what I was spending and saving (money, time and energy). It turns out there was a lot of camaraderie in what is at first glance an individual, personal project.

My ultimate purpose was big – I uncovered greater responsibility to myself and further reinforced my responsibility to others, to my own little ecosystem and to our planet. I hope you agree – we as humans are accountable for how we treat our earthly resources locally and globally. I discovered surprising and rewarding ways to increase my social influence. I realized I was overspending my time and my energy on way too many commitments outside my job and feeling tapped out. A few of the projects, committees and relationships were easy to let go, while others required some deep thinking and purposeful pro/con conversations with friends in order to release them. Lots of questions and eventually the "right" answers...

Besides my meaning of life questions, I had quite a few logistical ones. I interviewed Terri to understand more about how she crafted her year – the pros, cons and her "do-over" wishes. Early in my Nothing New year, I investigated books, watched videos and listened to speakers who had undertaken similar experiments. This helped a little and as much as I knew I would benefit from even the tiniest amount of planning, I still forged ahead without a real PLAN and let things unfold organically. Perhaps the resulting 12 months turned out to be more interesting because I did not do a lot of planning. I mapped things out as I went along and was more open to feedback and ideas from others in the process. Does NOT having a plan freak you out a little bit? I understand!

My year was different than Terri's and no doubt your year would be different than mine. I was energized by the spontaneous start to my Nothing New Year but you may need to do a little more planning. You might decide a year is too long for any number of reasons and craft a 3 month, 1 month or 1 week challenge. You may need to engage family members in the experience and/or explain to friends or colleagues what you plan on doing. In retrospect, it is essential to really solidify your purpose before moving ahead. It will be up to you to customize the experience for yourself and totally up to you to step over numerous reasons why now is not the right time. You know what I'm talking about – every new endeavor has a ramp up period. Then at some point you start. My gut feeling is you start today and then make do from here – not go on a stock-up-for-a-year shopping spree which would defeat the purpose. I think you would find, as I did, in almost every aspect of your life, you do indeed have everything you need and more!

You may want to set up some challenges or specialty months/ weeks to stay motivated. I started "Motivation Months" in June because once the new habits of Nothing New were established, I realized I had to keep things switched up a little to maintain momentum. My first Motivation Month was No Lights (about a 7 on a 10 point scale in terms of difficulty) and July was No Plastic...(almost impossible). August was Local Food, September was Greening My Cleaning, October and November were all about further detoxing with Natural Beauty Products. I spent December creating Handmade Gifts, did a Fashion Fast in January, a Trash Reduction in February and a Transportation Transformation in March. All with varying levels of success. I found there had to be some level of challenge (pain?) to make the experience significant.

The following 11 chapters are organized as a toolkit and arranged in a different order than my actual year played out. Some of my challenges and changes took more than one month and some less. I hope this framework will offer you a feasible yet challenging "how-to" for your own Nothing New experiment. In each section, I offer you my experience, the resulting learnings and some thought-provoking questions with space for you to write your ideas, plans, concerns, questions and lessons learned.

1. Stop Shopping
2. Grow Some Food
3. Eat Local
4. Buy Local
5. Turn Off The Lights
6. Consume Less Plastic
7. Detox Yourself
8. Make Stuff
9. Clean Your Closet
10. Track Your Trash
11. Guzzle Less Gas

Anytime I bought something outside my boundaries for the particular Motivation Month (happened a few times in a fit of forgetfulness/weakness), I put the specific dollar amount into a separate account to be donated at the end of the year. In addition, if there was a special coveted item I really wanted or almost bought, the equivalent dollar amount also went in. I called this my Nothing New Fund.

For example, I had collected mugs from a popular coffee chain over the years. The blue and white city mugs have a picture of the skyline and all kinds of great details about the location. An easy souvenir at $10.95 was a way to document places I'd been. My collection of 21 mugs is housed in the original built-in glass cabinets in my 1928 kitchen and serves as a memory lane conversation starter. These mugs are being replaced by a nice green and tan version but

I was always on the lookout for the discontinued blue ones. I was in San Francisco in April and I happened upon said coffee chain shop in the BART Station (Bay Area Regional Transportation) and saw the blue and white SF Skyline mug. Oh yay! Not knowing when (if) I would be back to SF, I picked up the mug, thinking I would make an exception this once. I set the mug on the counter and was ready to purchase. I guess it was pretty easy to slide off my year-long commitment since I was only a few weeks into it. I stepped back from the counter, put the mug back, gathered myself and decided NOT to buy it. I remember thinking, "If I am doing this then I am really going to do this." and moved on to meet a friend for lunch at the University of San Francisco.

I made the $10.95 count as my first contribution to the Nothing New Fund because I would have bought it if I were not doing this experiment. As a reward, I was available for a much cooler souvenir in being open to meet an amazing woman name Esther on the bus...launching the beginning of a shift in thinking on souvenirs in general. I kept track of new expenditures on the "allow" list to maintain the habit of high awareness of how I spend money. For example $350 worth of roofing supplies to fix my leaky porch roof was included. Reminder: I am thankful I have rarely have to worry about my basic needs.

For you, a Nothing New experience may increase your awareness and appreciation for what you have. It may offer you a whole new lifestyle or a subtle yet significant shift to living within your means. It may offer you alternatives to paying with credit and even help you pay off a debt. I hope you are inspired to do this – for a day, a month, a quarter or a year – and find out what happens.

Ready? Set? Go!

PONDER THIS...

- What might be compelling you to try Nothing New for yourself? Your household? Your family?

- What end result would you be hoping for and/or working toward?

- What were some of the messages you got growing up about buying things and saving money?

- Who do you need to get on board for a Nothing New challenge?

- In what areas of your life do you feel like you need a plan? Areas where you have been or want to be more spontaneous?

- Where in your life could you benefit from being more purposeful, mindful, aware?

Tools for Living Lean and Green

Stop Shopping
BUY TIME!

"Habit is necessary; it is the habit of having habits, of turning a trail into a rut that must be incessantly fought against if one is to remain alive."

**– Edith Wharton,
Pulitzer Prize-winning novelist (1862-1937)**

Here's the call – from the road, in the car, from Boston, "Hi, I've decided I am not going to buy anything new for one year." Pause. Silence. Then the mixed reviews. "Wonderful, yes, make it happen.", and "You need to write a book about it!" tempered with "It's about time." and "Really? You? Not shopping? Good luck." I extracted the positivity, dismissed the doubt and kept moving forward.

Many friends and family shared resources to give me ideas, hope and humility. We brainstormed about what the year could look like and got excited about the possibilities of what I might learn, how I could share my story and what this book might become. As I researched articles, websites and videos for inspiration on how to set up my year, I was humbled by the many people who seemed to be doing much more than I was about to do. Some were living in grass huts, had only 100 possessions, or were raising chickens, milking goats and making their own soap (Missy Martz!). Because I was sure none of these were going to be in my future, I used their stories as a benchmark. I would do the best I could to make the least impact possible with how I purchased goods, spent my money and managed my daily living.

Two main "aha resources" presented themselves early and helped convince me I could make some changes in my life, in my house and in my town to reduce the impact I was having with buying new things. More details here from my blog:

www. mostlynothingnew.blogspot.com:

Day 118 – July 25, 2010 – Sunday

I shared my Nothing New idea with Pat McCabe back on Day 6 while at the pivotal conference in Boston. She totally gets my plan and we had a great conversation about needs vs. wants, material things, consumerism gone bad and stuff in general. She mentioned a great resource, the *Story of Stuff* by Annie Leonard – viral video turned book – Pat used it to train her staff at the AMC (Appalachian Mountain Club). It tracks the manufacturing path of material things, explains planned obsolescence and our obsession with "things." It reinforced my feeling of obligation to spend, shop, live and work differently. Check it out. Have a Nothing New Day!

Ever since I learned about planned obsolescence in a memorable high school class called The City in my senior year (thank you Mr. Roever – where are you now?), I have been doing my best to take care of our planet earth. Done my share of worrying and thinking – maybe not enough doing. My Year of Nothing New really solidified my share of real work and action. Annie Leonard's work pulled everything together for me in a 20 minute video 31 years later. She points out the hidden flaws in the stuff we buy and highlights the good; how we are all connected in this sometimes terrible and often beautiful mess of a world. Her stories about how our stuff turns into trash and how it affects children, families, communities and systems inspired me to be more sustainable on a personal, and professional level.

The other aha was reading *Animal, Vegetable, Miracle – A Year of Food Life* by Barbara Kingsolver in 3 days. The book completely changed the way I viewed nutrition and the power/pleasure of eating locally and seasonally. Except she raised turkeys – I do not raise fowl nor will I – ever – oh and heads up if you are even a little squeamish, skip the chapter on "harvesting" turkeys. Thank you for sharing your copy with me Shelby Radcliffe!

Humor inspiration on stuff helped – I like comedian George Carlin's idea of a house being a "pile of stuff with a cover on it"...funny and true. We tend to fill the space we have AND much of the stuff we fill our spaces with is non-essential. Please don't misunderstand, I appreciate the memories, joy and beauty our stuff can bring. It may be a useful exercise to explore what value the stuff brings to you and how much stuff is "enough."

With these tools, loads of support and a beginner's mind, I started.

The first new habit was to completely stop going to the places allowing my spending temptation to triumph over shopping discipline unless it was for my essential living existence. The nearby mall and a few select stores were my trouble spots – you know you have your favorites! In addition to changing my shopping behavior and the commitment to not buy anything new, I needed to put some parameters around what I could and could not buy. Stephen Covey, author of *7 Habits of Highly Effective People*, says it takes 21 days to embed a new habit. It took me about 6 weeks to get used to the idea of not shopping. I eventually made peace with the new normal and got comfortable living without the little extras I had been incredibly free to purchase prior. In that time period, it became crystal clear I had enough – more than enough – to live, work, and play.

Most significantly, the ideas and questions around enough brought my privilege awareness into full focus. It ramped up in the beginning of my Nothing New Year as I started to scale back and consume more consciously. I realized more and more how much I already HAVE while faced with daily decisions on balancing what I WANT with what I NEED. I had always been appreciative of my opportunities and the resulting access I had been afforded and this was taking things to a whole new level.

Surely, my version of "living without" was on a very different level than many people I have met around Rochester and around the world. Someone who lives with their family of four in an apartment half the size of my house, someone who takes the bus out of necessity, or someone who relies on the kindness of others for every meal they eat. Someone who lives in a two-room structure with cardboard walls and a dirt floor and never once apologizes for what could seem like a lacking situation. Someone whose outrageous medical bills meant selling every possession became the only option to make ends meet. I am at times reluctant to tell my story, which in comparison to many other's is an easy story to tell. Perhaps some of these friends, neighbors or strangers would deem my comments, ideas or experience here as ignorant, fluffy or out of whack. My awareness of the blessings in my life is on high alert! What I have and who I am gives me incredible opportunity in the world. I have enough and in fact more than I will ever need. Gratitude, humility and learning rule the day.

As long as I'm oversharing, let me tell you I have discipline issues and difficulty doing things in moderation. The beginning of this endeavor was particularly challenging for me. It was a snap decision and a sharp left turn change in my behavior and I was not sure I could predict success. By June, I had 40 days of NOT shopping underway and it finally felt like this had become my new way of living. You too may struggle with the discipline of not shopping or in other areas of your life. I understand! It takes me a while to change behaviors even when I know it is good for me in the long run. There are several items with which I cannot be trusted unless I root myself in preventative habits. Let's say, for example, the issue is chocolate chip cookies, then better to avoid the cookie aisle in the store and make a good decision there then have to listen to the darn things calling out from the cupboard. Last count at my Wegman's – a family owned grocery chain in the Northeast/Mid-Atlantic US – there were 102 brands of cookies and that spells trouble. This is only an example, I of course have never struggled with this choc-full-o-chips situation. OK – back to not shopping...

I did a few other things to keep me honest and focused. I gave away the department store, clothing store or house store coupons I received in the mail, immediately recycled any and all catalogs and got obsessed about getting off mailing lists, all in the name of temptation management. It got easier to push shopping as an activity to the periphery and eventually completely out of the picture. I told a lot of friends what I was up to which meant there was a lot of support to balance out the challenges.

What I realize now is I was essentially crafting a new lifestyle not unlike the process of implementing new fitness and nutrition routines; it is hard to start then easier to maintain once the new way takes root.

The second step was to decide what Nothing New was actually going to mean for me and what I was going to allow – or not – in terms of purchases for my ongoing existence. I excluded any new clothing – second hand was OK but I limited it too – clothing was my downfall. In addition to no new clothing, there would be no new shoes, jewelry, or gifts for friends and family. My "kitty sitter" Hannah Galan would not be receiving her usual presents along with her cat-care fee (she was fine with it of course). No new flowers or plants for the house or for others (went to see Mom in person for Mother's Day instead of sending flowers – yay). No house décor, storage boxes, garden tools (or cute garden-y knick knacks). No new books, greeting cards, magazines, or writing journals (see "Box of Blank Journals" in the garage). Wanted a new phone – nope. Really wanted a new computer...say no. The focus would be on the basic needs – all of which were being met for me on a regular basis, I wasn't noticing like I thought I should…

ALLOWANCES

As Terri did, I set parameters for my Year of Nothing New. There are details on all of these allowed items in each of the Tools Sections. Being self-employed and solely responsible for maintaining my living, working and traveling life, I decided it was important to have the year be challenging without being so extreme it became a barrier. Your "allow list" would probably look different than mine and you would find the right balance of challenge for yourself. Here are the categories I thought about to set some boundaries for the year:

1. Food
I think all food is new because it is inherently a consumable product. I did two food-related challenges which really changed my outlook on how what I eat and where it comes from affects the planet and me. I worked hard to stick to a budget and to eat fresh whenever possible – not processed, prepared or pre-packaged.

2. Clothing
Only second hand and ONLY if I really needed it. We have numerous second hand stores in my town, which made it easy. I tracked my expenditures from the year prior and compared them to my Nothing New Year. Raised eyebrows. Check out the Epilogue for Year Two and Beyond.

3. Shelter – Electricity/Gas and Home Maintenance
For heating and cooling my house/office – a consumable. Again some cost savings by paying strict attention to my consumption of these items. I work out of the house and deemed it essential to have the "shelter" working smoothly.

I allowed necessary house repair items only if needed and repurposed if possible. I did end up needing to take care of a few things around the house. Many of the materials and equipment were new out of necessity such as shingles and a water heater. I allowed these for safety and security and for the integrity of my house.

4. Transportation – Car Repair/Gas

Gas is consumable and therefore must be bought new. I travel thousands of miles for work and I deemed this a necessity. I got good at shopping around for the best price thanks to the Gas Buddy app on my phone. If used parts were not available or appropriate (e.g. tires), I allowed new.

5. Work

I needed office supplies to run my business. I paid attention to these consumables in a way to be most cost effective and environmentally responsible. Using recycled paper, reusing paper and a gradual minimizing and elimination of giveaways at programs were part of the plan. Flash forward to the Leadership Lessons section for some surprising positive learnings and major changes on how I run Teamworks...financially and philosophically!

6. Personal/Home Care – Toiletries/Household Goods

These are also consumable and meant to be used. Streamlining personal and cleaning products ended up being a significant challenge to meet all of my criteria (no animal testing, recycled/recyclable packaging, locally made).

7. Experiences

My family is scattered in WI and FL so I allowed air travel for this year beyond what was required for work. I omitted concerts, shows and other entertainment events with a cost associated.

8. Gifts

Nothing for myself – for others only – second-hand, food items, or crafts hand-made by me.

Anything not on this list waited until March 20, 2011 or later. What I did not know at the time was the elimination of "shopping" would open doors I didn't even know I was standing in front of...

HOW TO...

1. Determine and affirm your shopping/spending hot spots – stores, brands, destinations...

2. Decide and commit to a timeframe of avoiding those hotspots – A week? A month? A year?

3. Set other parameters for your Nothing New – what you will allow/avoid.

4. Engage support from friends and family.

5. Document your learnings, savings, affirmations and revelations.

PONDER THIS...

- If you could change one thing about your shopping/spending habits right now, what would it be?

- What does the experience of buying non-essential things bring you/offer you?

- What aspects of your life might change with a Nothing New experiment?

- How would you share your one-minute response to "why are you doing this?" Guaranteed, someone will ask!

- How have you managed in the past with having to wait for rewards or accomplishments?

- What is "enough" for you?

Grow Some Food

HAPPINESS IS 123 PEAS

"I once had a sparrow alight upon my shoulder for a moment, while I was hoeing in a village garden, and I felt that I was more distinguished by that circumstance than I should have been by any epaulet I could have worn."

**– Henry David Thoreau,
Philosopher/historian (1817-1862)**

Before you skip this Tool because you have killed a houseplant or five in your past, let me assure you – you can grow something! You may be saying out loud to yourself, a family member, a roommate or a pet, "I barely have time to buy food much less grow it, get real lady." I understand AND I propose that you can grow a tomato plant or some lavender/mint/basil in your room, apartment or house easily. As a quick preview for Tool #3…If you can't grow something (lack of time, resources, space, energy, knowledge) then buy local/ seasonal as much as you can from a small grocer or farm stand. If not possible, then favor farm-grown over factory-made. To be clear, any food called by a name recognized around the world, coming through your car window, or turning your cereal milk a color (except blueberries) is an "edible, food-like substance", not actual food, as Michael Pollan names it, author of *In Defense of Food: An Eater's Manifesto*. More on local eating later…

Prior to the Nothing New year, I would not AT ALL have considered myself a gardener. I remember having a small garden on the side of the garage when I was little and recent talks with

Mom have confirmed as such. Maybe this new-found interest was a return to those origins? Ultimately, gardening became a source of joy, peace, gratitude and motivation during this year. It changed everything in terms of how I viewed "groceries."

I grew as much of my own food as possible which significantly altered my view of meal time. What I believe to be a God-given miracle of a lettuce seed the size of a pinhead turning into salad was Facebook status worthy. The life metaphors of how important seemingly insignificant things can be became part of my daily living and approach to how I cultivated my time, energy, money, and relationships. Big. Life-changing big. More on that later too.

In April of my Nothing New Year, I revived a garden space left by the previous owners and began the process of tilling, planting, and tending. Not fancy or magazine-cover-worthy this 14 x 5 foot area was bordered by metal stakes and square-holed wire. The door was fashioned out of said wire, an old piece of wood and a rusted latch that probably worked at one time. The door was more for the Gardener to feel happy about believing the door when closed would keep the rabbits (and groundhogs, and raccoons) out. To my surprise, there were no rabbit visitors (or their friends) to the garden of eatin' – only Japanese Beetles and squash bugs.

The plastic cover on the ground inside of the garden was held in place by rocks and roots. It took days to extract. Meant to deter weeds, the cover had become infused into the dirt and shredded itself as I pulled it out inch by inch. I had envisioned the simplicity of starting in the corners and pulling it up and off as easily as fluffing a tablecloth. Nope. I am pretty sure I lost a few fingerprints in this process. Embedded in the dirt were large plastic bowls to contain the extra-energized overzealous spearmint and chives. I chipped those out bit by bit – over the years, the plastic had become hardened and brittle. What I thought would be a "bend and snap" to extract the bowls turned into a project lasting an entire afternoon. This is when I began to really value the time it takes to have a garden – and

I had not even planted anything yet. Gratefully, I had the freedom to make the time to do this – it became a major project and even a hobby. Eventually, it was a motivator for managing my time to allow me to be out into my garden for at least an hour or two every day. It forced me to use the daylight hours very efficiently.

There were many long days (and nights) of cleaning up this area long neglected and overgrown. A few times I was out past sundown with my headlamp on, planting seeds or picking weeds in the windows of time I had between work trips and family visits. Night gardening is extra exciting to be sure – in the cold, early spring especially – many creatures are beginning to stir again. I felt almost camouflaged in the garden at night – and a little worried the neighbors would think me odd for being out there in the dark. I was fairly new to my street at the time and wanted to make a good impression yet the garden had to happen on its timeline not mine.

What to plant, what to plant? Once the area was cleaned up, I started educating myself on what would grow in my area. Until then, I had never fully appreciated the simplicity of the little map on the back of seed packets with instructions of where and when to plant. I mapped out the garden, tapped my inner Laura Ingalls Wilder (for the younger set – I am referencing the books and the TV show *Little House on the Prairie* – look for reruns on the Hallmark Channel) and started the process.

And, of course, thanks to the internet with its over abundance of information about gardening – a great place to start – *www. PickYourOwn.org*. I combined real life advice from real people at our local garden stores and even at Home Depot and I was on my way to becoming a "Gardener" with a capital "G". Most significantly, I was blessed with the friendship of two expert farmers, Fimka and Larry Cooley, at the Fairport Farmer's Market. They shared their knowledge and wisdom freely and answered all my questions with joy.

I learned everything I thought I needed to know and figured out what to plant: I decided on peas, lettuce, lima beans, tomatoes, basil, catnip, and squash. The spearmint and chives continued to grow themselves. I built four raised beds – two by eights and two by twos for this first year, which turned into quite a project. The wood was repurposed and the brackets/screws and the dirt were all new (see Nothing New Fund) while the bag of Popsicle stick garden markers were $.50 at Craft Bits and Pieces. I inherited a used compost bin (thanks Joe O'Gorman) and witnessed the exciting process of decomposition first hand. Happiness is a steaming compost bin in January!

The daily tasks of watering and weeding this little spot next to my garage transformed into a healthy garden patch. As it got warmer, the sweat dripping down my back, the dirt under my fingernails and the buzz of mosquitos all became part of the process. In the end, much of the crop yielded only small amounts – barely enough to enjoy at the time and definitely not enough to store. Darn. I had smug visions of a full freezer with garden goodies filling every niche – hopes of joining in Fall conversations with fellow gardeners, reminiscing about what had been canned, frozen and pickled to bring out in a glorious February celebration of the previous growing season. A Gardener nonetheless.

I was still quite proud of my peas and lima beans and as things progressed I gathered data on what to grow or not to grow in Year Two. As I mentioned, *Animal, Vegetable, Miracle* was a motivating factor in my garden beginnings. Most known for her novels, Barbara Kingsolver documented lessons on "deliberately eating food produced from the same place where we worked, went to school, loved our neighbors, drank the water and breathed the air." Barbara and her family lived off their own-grown products in the vicinity of their farm in VA. Very inspirational...In addition to sharing their wonderful story, she shares valuable facts about farming, in particular the impact of our nation changing dramatically from a rural to urban focus in a very short time.

I decided to skip new-not-planted-by-me decorative plants and flowers but new seeds would be OK. I transplanted some things from around the yard to fill out the garden in the front of my house – the Lambs Ear (soft fuzzy leaves and little yellow flowers) from out in the grass near the street grew as tall as I am. Other transplants like Forget-Me-Nots took as well. Thankfully, prior owners had done a fantastic job with perennials. I learned my neighbors (Marcia Brooks!) were keen on sharing – all of the Black-Eyed Susan patches on our street originated from one yard – thanks Joetta Keber! I decided I would never talk on my cell phone, or listen to music in the garden – out of respect for the peas of course. This became a place of uni-tasking – only gardening – and that was enough.

The focus on Kristin-Grown-Food and the local/seasonal eating focus carried over into the rest of the year – and a cookbook was in the works – "Kristin Kooks." I became increasingly appreciative and much more selective in the store. Fortunately, my friendship with Flmka and Larry (F&L) continued and I met them many Saturdays to pick up fresh, seasonal veggies – it was like a personal farm share. Maybe you can check your local Find A Farmer resource and join this thrilling movement?

A single tomato plant or herbs in a pot is easy – ready-made kits from a farmer's market, garden store or box store are OK. Container, dirt, and seeds included – add water, repeat and enjoy. The multiple benefits will satisfy several needs – the satisfaction of growing something, the marvel of a seed tuning into food, cleaner air in your living space, a fresh addition to your plate – and, a little bit of homegrown basil on your sandwich could contribute to world peace!

A bit more from my blog…some of my ponderings as I continued to bond with my garden, my yard and my little patch of the earth…

DAY 231 – November 15, 2010 – Monday
Snow's a Coming...

Prepping for our favorite season here in Rochester – we call it "The Winter" or "I'll See You When the Sun Comes Back Out in May." I finally cleaned out the small garden in the front of my house. I'd let it go free willy since August and there were many a random item including a small tree and a spiky tropical-looking plant I had no memory of whatsoever. Lots of holes in the dirt – buried squirrel treasure – and a ton of dead leaves. There are no trees right above this garden and I am not sure where said leaves came from – strange. A real mystery. By the way, rumor has it October was Squirrel Awareness Month – another mystery. Not to be confused with National Squirrel Appreciation Day on January 21st. As I was cutting, pulling and pondering how I was going to fit garlic planting into my day tomorrow, I got to thinking about a great chat I had with some conference attendees on Saturday about Nothing New. It is a unique conversation starter. I always appreciate what others know and are doing in their lives to cut back, cut down, or take out. Every small change, habit or effort is significant. We exchanged ideas on food, cleaning products and health/beauty goodies. Snow soon according to the "weather chatter" but I saw 40s and 50s on the weather report? Hmmm – may still have time to paint the porch steps once more before the cold weather really arrives. I'd like a different color blue…will use up the paint from last year and start fresh next spring to do the porch floor too. Been thinking about doing another year of Nothing New...Have a Nothing New Day!

In addition to becoming a weather nerd as a new Gardener, I was most excited by the number of peas I found in my garden. In spite of planting my peas way too late, there were a few pods – with anywhere from one-four peas inside. I had no idea on the timing thing never mind that peas grow on a vine and need a trellis of some sort to keep them organized – who knew? The pods yielded only 123 peas (about 1/4 cup) and it took me almost 10 minutes to shell. I will now look at a bag of frozen peas in a whole new light. The saying, "two peas in a pod" has extra meaning now. What will I plant next year? The US Census Bureau says nearly a quarter of us in the US grow some of our own food…what can you grow?

HOW TO...

1. Determine the size space you have to grow something – dill on the windowsill, peas in a pot, garlic in a garden plot?

2. Know your growing Zone and note any complications/ obstacles (like certain trees affecting the soil pH).

3. Decide what you want to grow and how – seeds for salad or salsa garden, prepped seedlings for veggies/ fruit? Yum.

4. Obtain the supplies (within your budget) – potting soil helps and raised beds (or planters) help keep things contained.

5. Plant On! Check the timing of the growing season for your area and become a weather geek to predict the last frost.

PONDER THIS...

- What would you have to do to have access/ability to grow where you live and work?

- What kind of food was in your household growing up? What was that like?

- What is your favorite vegetable or fruit? Can you grow it in your yard or living space?

- What kind of homemade goodies do you most like to receive from someone else?

- Who do you know who grows some of their own food?

- Who can support your growing efforts? Whose efforts can you support – individuals or organizations?

Eat Local

WHAT'S IN YOUR BACKYARD?

"Shake the hand that feeds you."

**– Michael Pollan,
Author**

People were most curious about what I ate during my Year of Nothing New more than any other feature of this experience. "What about food?" I had assembled a respectful response of, "I had a vegetable garden, ate only NY State produce for one month and am working hard at being a localvore to live, work, shop and eat within a 100 mile radius. I had to eat new food, because when it's used it is gone..." I think they were really asking about prepared meals and eating in restaurants, which I did to some degree with certain parameters (local/non-chain). As a result of having a garden, I began to re-see food as wonderful fuel for my body to allow me to do what I need to do. As reward (ice cream), punishment (why?) or decoration/celebration (birthday cake) is OK – in moderation. More than ever though, I thought about and appreciated who grew the zucchini, who weeded the brussels sprouts, and who packed and shipped the carrots to my Wegman's.

I am certain things happen for a reason and we are all somehow woven into the same web. In relation to growing and eating homegrown and homemade food, I was completely sold on the value of knowing where everything came from. There was plenty to eat in my backyard – not literally – I would need more than the wild raspberries growing out in the back or the black walnuts dropping from my six tall trees each fall. But, what if there was enough to eat within 100 miles of where I (you) live?

I decided my Motivation Month for August was to eat only foods grown in NY State. I became a "Localvore-In-Training" and started researching what there was to eat within my 100-miles. August is one of my busiest travel months. The caveat was as I moved about the country, I would eat only food grown in the state I was in AND not eat in any restaurants at all. I was in NY for the most part with a few trips into MA, PA and NH. I ate a lot of corn and potatoes to be sure. Oh and apples, arugula, beets, black beans, blueberries, broccoli, cabbage, cantaloupe, carrots, cauliflower, chard, cucumbers, currants, eggplant, garlic, green beans, kale, lettuce, nectarines, onions, peas, peaches, pears, plums, radishes, raspberries, spinach, squash, tomatoes, watermelon, and zucchini. Add in Chobani Greek Yogurt made in NY, local honey and maple syrup and I think that answers the question about "enough." I was able to find local flour and eggs – for a higher price and worth it to me. Even tried a duck egg – very interesting. I will stay with chicken eggs for the long term. I tried Jerusalem artichokes (yum), beet greens, carrot greens and leeks (no, no and no thank you) as part of this month's experiment. I attempted to make tea with the carrot tops based on someone's entry on a food website. Safe to eat apparently but unless you like brown-green dirt water, I do not recommend this. I will not judge you. Nonetheless, happy me, to have the means and the access for this.

Why bother with fresh, local food??? The Center for Urban Education for Sustainable Agriculture (CUESA) estimates the average American meal travels about 1500 miles to go from farm to plate. This is problematic for several reasons:

"This long-distance, large-scale transportation of food consumes large quantities of fossil fuels. It is estimated we currently put almost 10 kcal of fossil fuel energy into our food system for every 1 kcal of energy we get as food. Transporting it over long distances also generates great quantities of carbon dioxide emissions. Some forms of transport are more polluting than others. Airfreight generates fifty times more CO_2 than sea shipping. Sea shipping is slow, and in our increasing demand for fresh food, it is increasingly being shipped by faster – and more polluting – means. In order to transport food long distances, much of it is picked while still unripe and then gassed to ripen after transport, or it is highly processed in factories using preservatives, irradiation, and other means to keep it stable for transport and sale. Scientists are experimenting with genetic modification to produce longer-lasting, less perishable produce."

Closer is better! With my new-found awareness of the absolute phenomenon of how food is grown I continued to educate and train myself on being a localvore. Prior to starting my Nothing New Year, I was still eating chicken and fish but complicated matters more by becoming mostly vegetarian as time went on.

Throughout this special year, I continued to get to meet with college student leaders from all over the United States and I got to go to Rivier University in NH three to four times a year. At a retreat in my NN Year, a new friend, Spencer asked us at lunch "Who wants to see pictures of our family dressed as pirates with chickens on our shoulders?" (a Johnny Depp reference). My answer was, "Yes please." and from there I learned more about his mom Wendy Thomas and what they all do as a family to conserve, live simply and eat locally. Inspiring. Wendy has trimmed her weekly grocery bill for their family of 8 (6 kids and 2 adults) to $140, yes, that's right $140. Check out her blog *Lessons Learned from the Flock* and read about her methods, her family and her chickens.

It seems obvious now – local, seasonal, organic is fresher, safer and better tasting. It has not been sprayed, colored or oiled, is often less expensive, uses fewer resources and supports the local economy. According to *Animal, Vegetable, Miracle*, if everybody in America ate one local, organic meal per week, we would cut the nation's oil consumption by 1.1 million barrels a week. New York Times columnist Mark Bittman is an expert in this area. He busts a popular myth with his article, *Is Junk Food Really Cheaper?"* as a challenge for us to check facts and do the research on what we eat. Solid action happening across the United States now to counteract food deserts with urban garden awareness, education and financial sourcing. Ron Finley in Los Angeles, CA is "planting the seeds and tools for healthy eating" and Will Allen's movement *Growing Power* in Milwaukee, WI is leading the way in building "sustainable, equitable and ecologically sound food systems." Fabulous. My next venture will be to join up with our own *Rochester Roots* to play a role in their mission of "creating a locally sustainable food system". Plenty of work to be done and endless ways to be involved.

Yay for local, seasonal, organic, homegrown! I started cooking and baking a lot more in this month. I made a local peach pie for a friend with a crust from scratch – took way more time than taking a crust out of the freezer yet comforting to know there were four simple ingredients – flour, sugar, salt and butta. ☺ Canning now has a place in my heart. New York peaches, concord grape jam and strawberry jam line my pantry shelves ready to be enjoyed come February. I have perfected a few other homemade goodies, many with locally grown ingredients. Pesto, hummus, baba ganoush (eggplant spread), granola, and gluten-free zucchini bread (as of 2013, I am mostly wheat-free) all make me happy. I will share.

Simple, did not mean easier. It did take a lot more time to plan and prepare – here is a blog entry from August:

Day 126 – August 2, 2013 – Monday
Learning Curve

I underestimated how significant of a change this month of NY foods is going to be. I thought I was all set to go then it turns out I have to be very deliberate about prep and follow through. Saying this after making pesto at 2 in the morning because I picked it and did not want to waste it. Planning Ahead is going to be Habit Number One in my Localvore series! Found out today that although Wegman's makes most of their own bread, the flour comes from Idaho. Do I mention them enough? They should be my blog sponsor. NY produces flour here somewhere apparently not in a large enough quantity to be cost effective – therefore, Idaho wins the Flour Derby...bummer. Now there's nothing wrong with Idaho, I will just need to decide how far I want to go with this NY thing. Does It have to have all NY INGREDIENTS? Locally made bread is still better than it being made somewhere else and shipped to my area. Will check out Lori's Natural Foods ASAP for some ideas. I packed my meals for several days – hope it lasts me – realizing I am in dire need of more reusable containers. Will have to look around at yard sales for "new" ones because am not a fan of buying used storage containers. More later as I entertain possible reactions from bringing endless containers of vegetables – stay tuned. Have a Nothing New Day!

A 3 day retreat with York College in early August was my first road trip test with all my own food. Luck would have it for me to find a refrigerator in our meeting room. I kept everything right there and didn't have to store anything in the retreat site kitchen, thus going mostly unnoticed with my multiple containers. I did not want people to think I didn't like what they were serving. I kept explaining what I was doing, which seemed to ease things. I was worried for nothing because most everyone there either didn't notice and if they did they were interested in what I was doing.

As the month progressed, I discovered eating too many vegetables was not necessarily a good thing. I struggled in a personal veggie land attempting to be vegetarian. It was not working for me! Days into it and I was having nightmares about eating beets – not OK. I really needed to find an eating balance with a little less fiber and a little more protein. Protein is a concern because I really shouldn't eat soy, or peanuts which made me think intensely about locally grown beans (in my free time). I know my protein need is real – and very related to my thyroid issue. Don't worry – I am not about to share ALL my internal health issues with you in what my dad used to call an "organ recital" – get it? Hee hee.

When I had almost given up on finding black beans grown in NY State, there was a ray of hope this past weekend. The belief of "no local black beans" was bringing me down. Based on the research I had done, I really thought black beans were not grown here. Perhaps I should have tried harder. I needed to forgive myself and move on. As I was mentioning my protein/black bean woes to some lifetime Rochesterians one Saturday, I received this response, "What? We have black beans here, what do you mean you can't find black beans grown in NY?" He was a bit upset and in total disbelief, as if I had suggested paper is made from cheese. He gave me the farm name and the farmer's name. That was easy. The NBBINY (No Black Beans In NY) myth was busted. Right up there with the Easter Bunny and dying from eating fizzy candy and drinking a brown carbonated beverage, the No Black Bean myth was debunked. With a little research on the internet, I found my source. One phone call to John at NY Beans and I was on my way to buy 25 pounds of black beans grown in my 100 mile radius. Woo hoo!

This local food thing became a personal movement for me – much inspiration came from reading, talking and listening and I realized (even said out loud to myself) all the good food in my fridge does not leave room for any junk. Imagine. FOOD COMES FROM FARMS.

HOW TO...

1. Find your local farmer's market, CSA (Community Supported Agriculture) and/or farm share.

2. Know the source of your food – closer is better.

3. Eat one meal a week consisting only of local/seasonal/ organic.

4. Buy local produce whenever possible – farm grown trumps factory made.

5. Stock your freezer – preserve your local produce easily for enjoyment later.

Bonus: You can put zucchini in almost everything (thank you Shelby).

PONDER THIS...

- What "abundance" is in your 100-mile radius?

- What do you know about your favorite food?

- What are your food luxuries? Avocados from Peru, bananas from Columbia? Any kind of chocolate?

- What percentage of the food in your pantry, cupboard, fridge, dining hall is processed vs. fresh/single ingredient?

- Do you know how your food has been grown or altered in color, flavor or shape?

- How much of your total budget is spent on food?

Buy Local

It's Good Business

"We envision a thriving, collaborative community where local businesses are prosperous, and contribute to a healthy environment and the well being of all citizens."

– Economic Forum for Building Sustainable Communities

Buying and eating local led to a focus on buying other things locally. Granted I wasn't buying much, but it showed up in other ways such as avoiding chain restaurants and coffee spots, department stores and malls in favor of local businesses and shops. My biggest downfall is clothing and avoiding the mall, where there are only new items to be purchased from national stores, took the temptation right off my plate. Questions about clothing were popular – friends asked with wonder and amazement how I could go a year with no new shoes. Because I had decided early on this would be the case, it was easy to stick to.

A student at Arizona State asked a thought provoking question during a talk I was giving about Nothing New while I was in Year Two. She wanted to know if I thought I was negatively affecting the economy with my not buying anything new. I was flattered she thought I had some impactful influence. It was a great question and I had been asked at least once before. Before I share my answer, know this particular leadership conference was sponsored by a major department store. I felt it was important to give a polite, respectful and truthful answer to the question. The small local businesses, farmers, artists and chefs I was shopping with and buying from <u>are</u> part of the economy. Secondhand and consignment stores, local pubs, and soap makers were all contributing – as was I, being their customer. Albeit contributing in a different way from shopping in the national name stores. "I love (insert name of major department store)!", I explained. "I didn't go there for a while, that's all."

The department store representative guy was no longer making eye contact with me at this point. A picture of his store and the company logo were in my slide presentation. Awkward. If only I had a do-over...Ouch. I was as transparent and genuine as I could be. The rest of my talk was fine – lots of other questions and quality time with a group of talented college students. And it got me thinking more about THE ECONOMY...

An article in Time Magazine from June 2009 spelled out multiple benefits of buying local. More money stays in the community, you can be more certain of what you're getting, increased local/regional resilience, and local jobs were among the benefits. Buying local helps avoid what the author Judith Schwartz calls "clone-towns" where Main Street looks like Every Main Street with the same chain restaurants and shops. Money circulates more quickly with a local business base and can help a neighborhood, town or city stay stronger and withstand economic downturns. I am working hard to buy local to play a role in d) all of the above.

Oddly, my work life is not local at all. I work in my house for the most part (0 miles) then drive up to 8 hours (hundreds of miles) most times and often fly much further to my training programs. On one of those long drives to NH from Rochester, I had tons-o-time to think, dream and marvel at the lack of driving finesse on US highways. I actually saw a woman leaning back on her arm with her eyes CLOSED. For real. I honked at her and she woke up and showed me her angry eyes. I had the calm leisure of listening to some classic New England National Public Radio (NPR always seems hipper in New England) and got inspired by the idea of a "Six Word Memoir"...Probably the most famous of these is from novelist Ernest Hemingway when asked to write a six word novel, "For Sale: baby shoes, never worn." In that spirit, the book *Not Quite What I Was Planning* by author Rachel Fershleiser is a collection of six word memoirs. When I got back I ordered the book (used, of course) and quickly read it cover to cover. Some of them are clever, some humorous, some sad...Here are few of mine from a NH road trip – in the spirit of Nothing New as in less can indeed be more and there are no real rules – one or several six word memoirs a day (or in your life) is perfectly acceptable, offered freely and of course, never judged...

Malted milk eggs not as hoped.

Overnight success fifteen years of toil.

Choices made vulnerable life of love.

Rooted in faith free to live.

You know it's gonna be alright.

Enough in the garden is enough. (Deep, I know)

Year Two was a continuation of my momentum – I decided to start swimming again. I would buy the necessary equipment from a small swim shop vs. online. Technically, Mary Jones' store D&J Sports is not local to me here in NY but she is a fellow small-business owner friend in Lewisburg, PA. Here is a blog entry from Year 2....

DAY 400 – April 22, 2011 – Friday
Swimming Pending New Suit Still Needed
(Today's Six Word Memoir)

I am afraid the "six word memoir" concept has taken over my brain. Will use in moderation I promise (6 words). I have decided to start swimming again after watching my nephews Jonathan and Alexander in a couple of meets now. Jon is GOOD and I'm not saying it because he is my relative and gets all his talent from me. His brother Alexander is younger and he is going to be quite a swimmer too – maybe a diver? I have accompanied them to early Saturday morning practices. I have watched them prep mentally for the meet while their mom Glenda writes the event/lane/heat on their arms with a Sharpie. I have observed the pre-race cap/goggles/shake out the arms and legs ritual, and I have cheered them on for the brief seconds they fly, stroke, and freestyle their way to the finish. Along with flashbacks to my own high school swimming, a recent spotting of Olympic swimmer Dara Torres has propelled me to put my former-athlete self back into the pool. I am making the decision to by a new suit, cap and goggles – these are such personal items – therefore getting them used does not appeal to me. Got advice from Jon on what swimsuit to buy – he said green, black or blue is best. Starting May 18, 2011, I will head back into my second year of Nothing New fueled by renewed energy from the pool chlorine, gardening successes and the vision of further financial stability and freedom. Yay – Have a Nothing New Day!

Another part of my quest for local-ness was a search for local health and beauty and it took me two months to solidify. This was related to my efforts to detox my living space and my health.

As a preview for Tool #7, I met another friend, Mary Bartolotta, in October of 2010 and learned about her local business, Mooseberry Soap Company. Quality soap made in her factory located 2.52 miles from my house. Now that's local!

I continued to search for greener behaviors, cleaner methods, and local products to ultimately reduce my impact on the planet. I found a green dry cleaner called Martinizing for the few items I have dry cleaned – remember One Hour Martinizing? This is a ramped-up franchise version of the older company which now uses a process called Green Earth Cleaning. The owner, Todd Sankes, is a delight to speak with about being green. Prices are reasonable plus they take back hangers and the plastic bags for reuse and recycling. Like it. Right next door to Martinizing is the Ravioli Shop – guess what they sell. Yes. Local ravioli and rustic bread. Life is good. Another favorite local is Anything Goes – an attractive consignment store with beautiful owners Virginia Chiccino and Rhonda Miles – a 10 minute walk from my house.

My final frontier and slight obsession is products MADE IN THE USA. It was getting really uncomfortable to purchase and (usually) give away "Made in China" workshop tokens or team building items for Teamworks. This was especially true during my Year of Nothing New. Rubber chickens had become a bit of a trademark activity/giveaway for me and to some of my clients I was known as The Rubber Chicken Lady. We can debate this relevance in another book.

I needed beach balls frequently for certain activities too – all made in China – though the companies I would order from are based in NE or MI, the items themselves were traveling 7900 miles to arrive at my door from China. It was hard to justify and it made me really think about the importance of rubber chickens in the work I do. Hopefully, my reputation rests on something more solid. This was not an overnight phase out and shift to "Made in USA" as a mantra for Teamworks and to some degree is still a work in progress. I had a wake-up year in the evolution of my company about 10 years ago when I realized I spent almost $10,000 on giveaways at my programs. Not good. I understand we are in a global economy yet I can choose to foster a local business culture instead and green my own business in the process.

Back to local buying – I promise to wrap it back to the point of this Tool. We are fortunate to be able to buy things from all around the world and I expect there are hidden costs. On a personal buying level, when I buy something, I am in complete agreement with how it was made. The closer I am to the person who makes the soap, cleans the sweater, cooks the ravioli, or sells me the suit, the easier it is for me to be in agreement with all aspects of the final product. It makes the whole buying process much more personal, less anonymous. It is like knowing your neighbors on a level of going over for dinner – way beyond waving hello at the mailbox.

HOW TO...

1. Check out the local businesses in your 100-mile radius.

2. Decide what product features are most important to you, e.g. made in USA, organic, no animal testing, or ingredients source, whatever your hot button is...

3. Set a time period to "buy local" and document your experience, e.g. what you learn about business, money, entrepreneurship.

4. Discover other local businesses you could support, e.g. services, entertainment, clothing, crafts, technology.

5. Give coupons and catalogs for stores away – or find a way to craft a campaign or fundraiser with the coupons.

PONDER THIS...

- What are you willing to pay more for because it is local?

- What store/brand is your "hot spot" and could you avoid if for a year?

- When was a time you were caught off guard on an issue and defaulted to transparent and genuine?

- What is a Six Word Memoir describing your interest in Buying Local (or greening your life in some way)?

- Growing up, what are your memories of buying stuff – What stores? What products? What experiences?

- When have you felt totally in congruence with your beliefs and your behaviors? When have you felt totally out of whack?

Turn Off the Lights

CANDLELIGHT IS UNDERRATED

"It is well to be up before daybreak, for such habits contribute to health, wealth, and wisdom."

**– Aristotle,
Philosopher (384-322 BC)**

I have never been a morning person. Ever. I loved staying up late. Bragged about it. Have fond memories of eating cereal late at night at the kitchen table with Dad discussing current events, our family, and life in general...sigh. Hereditary, habit and emotional connections to the stay-up-late world determined my biorhythms early in life.

I had always certainly appreciated the sunrise from an intellectual point of view only – I understood how the earth turns and rotates around the sun and then it "comes up" to start the daylight process. I got how the morning has value for other people. I tried to understand the a.m. draw and would listen respectfully to all the Morning People who spoke words like (with a slice of smug might I say, which could have been my imagination), "It's the best part of the day", "I get so much done before everyone else is even out of bed", "I wake up ready to go" and "I love the peacefulness." You know who you are. These were the people who exercised in the morning, which was a complete mystery to me. I had been-there-done-that in college as a rower attending 5:30am practice (my last year of rowing by the way) – a very long time ago in a galaxy far away. I struggled with the early practice schedule and with other morning responsibilities of student teaching. Add to that my inevitable late night residence hall obligations as a House Fellow and how most of the incidents occurred after 11pm, helping foster my lack of appreciation for morning.

Fast-forward to my work life after college. My life as a late-nighter continued to perfect itself through grad school and into the beyond. I seemed to have a second wind around 10pm and was usually wrapping things up by 1:30am or so. Seems my most productive hours were say, 11am until 3pm when the caffeine wore off – then pick back up again around 6pm until midnight or 2am. If needed, I could stay up all night and secretly liked proving I could do it. I wore my night owl status like a Miss America sash. I envisioned myself among the proud few who dared to stay up once everyone else had gone to sleep. The "strong Norwegian woman, Midwest bred, do what you have to do and stay up until you finish it" persona ran all aspects of my life. My sister poet Edna St. Vincent Millay (Pulitzer Prize-winning poet (1892-1950) captured my lifestyle precisely:

> My candle burns at both ends;
> It will not last the night;
> But ah, my foes, and oh, my friends --
> It gives a lovely light! ("First Fig")

Being self-employed for the past 17 years meant I was free to burn the candle at both ends with my 11am-2am/14 hour workday with relatively little repercussion. I was cramming everything in, getting it all done, and making it all happen, or so I thought. I was running my business and traveling for work, creating some professional development opportunities for myself, and making some time to see friends and family who are scattered between MN, WI, OH, CO, FL, PA and NY. The hard part was being built as a marathoner trying to run my life as a sprinter. My post-travel recovery time was increasing and I was feeling like I was giving 10% to everything and 100% to nothing. Had I been in a traditional workplace, I am sure the odd schedule and increasing weariness would have warranted a letter in my file. The freedom I have to choose my work hours is' wonderful. I am pretty sure I will never go back to a 9-5 situation – most likely never – should always leave room for a Plan B!

When I started my Nothing New year, my stay up late/get up late approach had already started to lose its novelty – after all those years. Given the weird year prior and other various physical (aging) changes going on, it made sense I was in need of a change in my workday hours. Little did I know when I launched my first monthly challenge in June to turn off the lights, the process of shifting my working/waking hours would have a huge, positive effect on all other areas of my life. After the initial Stop Shopping, this was my first major monthly challenge.

Originally, I was going to set June up as No Electricity Month. Then I started listing the exceptions – refrigerator, computer, phone, and oh yeah it would be good to still use the washer and dryer, oh and the air conditioning. OK. After thinking about it for 7 seconds, I settled on No Lights/No Dryer Month. The right balance of challenging and doable. I hung everything out to dry around the house and on the laundry line outside my back door. A little more work for sure but I felt good about using a little less electricity. Since June has the longest days, I thought the no-lights thing would be easy. Fifteen hours of daylight seemed like more than enough. My "rules" were to leave the lights off for the month and use candlelight or flashlight when needed. I decided to allow the back porch light to remain on at night throughout the month for safety reasons – often my travel brings me back late at night and I wanted to maintain the light as a security feature.

On June 1, 2010, I started my day with excitement for the pending monthly challenge. I woke up about 7am and was on the road by 10am (I know – no big deal for the Morning People but for me to be upright, functioning and operating a motor vehicle all before noon was cause for a celebratory Tweet). I drove to New York City for a program at Pace University the next day. I arrived, checked in, parked and as I was walking into my room for the night, reached for the light switch. Ooops. Hmmm – I had not really thought through my no-lights rules for travel. I put my things down and donned my trusty headlamp – oh yes, I always travel with a headlamp! Don't you? Needless to say, using a flashlight in a hotel room seemed creepy. Plus it brought back some unpleasant memories of being in a hotel fire situation a few years back (no one was hurt – although I was pretty sure I was going to meet Jesus in the stairwell). After about 15 minutes of "this is weird" I decided I would adopt a one-light-rule for travel. Only one light on in the room at a time. Doable? Next time you are in a hotel, note how easy it is to have the bathroom light, the reading light AND the desk light on all at once without even thinking/blinking. It took several attempts to secure the habit of one light so within a few hours became the norm...way better than the headlamp.

I arrived back from this trip around 2am – the back porch light was on and I liked how much shine it gave off as I let myself in the door. I lit a few candles in the bathroom to wash up (helpful to see while flossing) and headed up to sleep. I was really tired from the drive from NYC, therefore no attempts to read by headlamp or candlelight this night.

With no lights to turn on, my working day was predetermined by the rising and setting of the sun. During June in the US Northeast the sun rises around 5:30am (5am is begin civil twilight aka "dawn") and sets around 9pm (light until 9:30pm aka end civil twilight aka "dusk"). My emerging workday would become dawn to dusk with much more time to do other things besides work!

Over the month I adapted to this schedule with a tiny initial trauma of letting go of my nighttime working hours. Little did I know "9-5" would become my sleeping hours. In the beginning, I tried to work past dusk with a variety of alternative light sources. Much of my work is on the computer – emailing, bookkeeping, writing – I thought it would be a cinch with the light of the computer screen. If you have ever tried to work on a computer in the dark, you know how looking at the screen makes the keyboard invisible when you glance down to check your ticky-typing (unless you have genius expert typing skills and do not have to look down – Mom this means you). After the fail, I tried to work by candlelight as a modern Abraham Lincoln who reportedly did his homework and reading by the light of the hearth. The romance was over on the Abe experiment in a flash. Not only was the candlelight insufficient wattage, my cats like to hang out wherever I am working and the candle "shrine" required to light my workspace was a true fire hazard for swishing cat tails. Not to mention I should not have been comparing Facebook by candlelight to laying the foundation for the Gettysburg Address by firelight.

Next up on trying to extend the day, deny the sunset, and control my work hours, was my handy headlamp, this time for actual work-use not maneuvering around my hotel room. This headlamp goes on all camping, driving, and flying trips. I am often accused of being a heavy travel packer partly because I have all the extras. I like my headlamp but it was not a solution here. The stream of light was horribly distracting, "look up, look down, up now down, now I am looking up, now I am looking down" – and was not allowing me to do any real work. Thank you anyway headlamp, go to your carry-on.

After a few days of this trial and error and a left-eye twitch, I started to let go of my work and the control by 9pm. This was against my grain yet it started to become enjoyable. It was motivating to focus on getting things done by a strict deadline everyday (sunset) – challenging initially because most of my deadlines are self-imposed/flexible given my self-employed career lifestyle. I did use candles occasionally to light my washing up activities and did try to read in bed, but the light of the flame was not enough and was surely a fire hazard. Soon, my "reverse 9-5" was in place and I got into a set of new habits. In thirty days, the 5am-9pm day gave me fresh perspectives on work, time, and priorities.

This from my blog…final day of No Lights Month…

Day 105 – July 1, 2010 – Thursday

Last day of no lights yesterday – good. It was challenging to be sure on a few levels and I learned a lot. Candle light is not very bright and it moves, light from the refrigerator lights only the kitchen sink area (and feels wasteful), "light" from my cellphone is non-useable, computer work in the dark is no good. I know where EVERYTHING is in my house now and am in a much better habit of going to sleep early. Finished up some laundry as I launch another road trip. Hung most of it all around my house – a good habit from my No Lights Month (which started out as no electricity month – not doable for me). I decided I always had to hang at least half on the line to dry. I still do this with every load. Towels and sheets, rugs and jeans were still hung up and hung out. Inherited a useful over the door rack-thing making it easy to hang shirts and tops too. Good. Along with flossing regularly after a "scared straight" talk from my dentist, you can call me Good Habit Girl. Have a Nothing New Day!

Oh and by the way, my June electric bill was ultra-low in comparison to the year prior – I did not turn on any lights except the back porch light at night to keep the Boogey Man away and in my office the night my printer crashed. My June 2010 bill was $18.40 June 2009 bill was $40.33. Of course there are a lot of variables here, weather, my travel schedule etc. Our electric is really cheap – my town/village has our own electric company overseen by a Municipal

Commission financed entirely by customer rates – excellent.

On this Nothing New journey, people offered their stories and experiences. A fellow passenger, Mary, in the Orlando airport shared with me she was not sure could do the no-lights thing. She liked to keep a light on in every room at night as a comfort thing. My friend Sue likes to "keep the home fires burning" with a small light on in the living room all night. I like having my back porch light for security. The flip of a switch is much more than making it "not-dark." Thanks to June 2010, I appreciate my lamps more (don't worry I do not thank them when I turn them on because it would be unusual), notice the calmness of the end of the day, the peace of a single lit candle and can have a conversation about the sunrise – having seen it in person on a regular basis!

HOW TO...

1. Decide what electricity/utility you can power down as a challenge for one month.

2. Solidify your "rules" for reducing the use of energy in your living space.

3. Align your waking/working life as closely as possible to your most productive hours.

4. Experiment with waking up earlier and going to bed earlier if you can.

5. Track your electricity/utility use to note financial savings.

PONDER THIS...

- What do you value most about your daylight hours?

- What would you be able to do differently if you changed your personal "rising and setting" times?

- What are your energy highpoints in the day?

- What are your habits around lights/energy use?

- What would be different for you if you could change your work hours?

- From what/where/whom do you gather comfort?

Consume Less Plastic

YOU ARE PROBABLY WITHIN AN INCH OF SOMETHING PLASTIC RIGHT NOW

"Every time you lay money down on the counter to buy something, you are saying, "I approve of this object. I approve of how it was made, the materials that are in it, and what's going to happen to it when I no longer need it and throw away."

– Gloria Flora,
Director of Sustainable Obtainable Solutions,
Former US Forest Service Coordinator

In addition to starting my blog in July, I needed a new challenge for the next month to take me deeper into the world of conscious consumption. Thought it would be intriguing to use nothing plastic for 30 days. I envisioned a life of tin foil, wax paper and reusable shopping bags but plastic is in everything and everywhere. Everywhere. In practically everything. As I was touching the fridge door handle (plastic), for a container of yogurt (plastic) to refuel and sit down to begin my blogger life at my computer (more plastic), I realized not using plastic would be almost impossible. My car has plastic in/on it as does my phone, watch, shower curtain, travel mug and many other daily use items. The cap on the OJ box, the little tab on the concentrated lemonade can, the handle on the natural kitty litter, the wrapper around the lid of the plastic container for the hummus…EVERYWHERE.

I know there are good uses for plastic – certainly in the medical world. Brings to mind other good uses – safety goggles, protective gloves, raingear – not sure how to make those without using plastic.

There are bad plastic uses in my opinion, ever present in the form of one-time-use items – cups, plates, utensils, fast food/take out packaging, actually most packaging.

Given the pervasiveness of plastic, I altered my July challenge to focus on not *buying* anything plastic. Still quite an experiment – could it be recyclable? No. The whole point was to REDUCE first, then Reuse, then Recycle. Now I Repair and Repurpose even before I Reduce. At the time, my town only recycled #1 and #2 plastics, as do most, and many containers/packaging shells out there are #5 and #6. It wouldn't really help with my recycling efforts anyway. I knew I would have a hard time finding recycling out there in airports and hotels. The whole point was to not buy the plastic in the first place. Good news is my county now recycles up to #7 – I sent a thank you note to Mike Garland, our County Director of Environmental Services, and got a prompt thank you letter back.

I was a little ahead of the game on No Plastic Month with a new-to-me To-Go Ware bamboo utensil set given to me in May by my new friend Gina Russo in Utah. She is a bicycle commuter and outdoor advocate. When Gina lived in Washington, DC she helped start one of the first CSAs (Community Supported Agriculture) in the US, growing 12,000 pounds of sweet potatoes one year on ¾ acre of land – oh my! She got rid of all plastic ware and Styrofoam cups in her office and personally carries her own utensils – a kit called "To-Go Ware"– spoon, fork, knife and chopsticks made out of bamboo in a little bag made out of recycled plastic on a mini-carabiner to boot.

As I was telling Gina about my Nothing New experiment over lunch at "The U," it was hard to focus as I was coveting her bamboo fork. I was thinking about how I could find a gently used set of these amazing utensils and I was about comment on it, when she said, "Here you can have mine, I'll buy another set for myself." So kind and generous, I almost fell out of my chair. Never will I eat another cup of instant oatmeal with a coffee stirrer in my hotel room – hooray! From then on, I would travel with my Fab Four – To-Go Ware, cloth napkin, water bottle and a travel coffee mug, carried in a little reusable nylon bag. I would not have to buy anything plastic – especially in the airport. Felt good AND still learning.

I travel for work – on trains, planes and automobiles – and this year in particular, there were a lot of planes. Don't even get me started on plastic/trash in airports and on airplanes. Oh, OK, I will start. According to the National Resources Defense Council (NRDC), "the US airline industry discarded 9,000 tons of plastic in 2004 and enough newspapers and magazines to fill a football field to a depth of more than 230 feet. Airports are responsible for a huge amount of trash—the 10 airports reporting waste generation data in our survey generated 1.28 pounds of waste per passenger in 2004, about one third of the total amount of waste Americans generate in an entire day. Most of the trash discarded at airports is sent to landfills and incinerators. At this rate of waste generation, the 30 largest airports in the United States generate an amount of waste equal to a city the size of Miami." Good news – it is improving as the awareness increases. Flash-forward to a spot on National Public Radio December 2012 – Charlotte Douglas International Airport now uses 1.9 million worms to eat through its organic waste. The airport has reduced the trash it sends to the landfill by 70 percent. I know this is a chapter on plastic, not worms...you know it's all related. And it gets better...there is now an indoor garden at Terminal 3 at Chicago O'Hare and supplies many of the restaurants in the airport. The 2013 *Recycling, Reuse and Waste Reduction at Airports* report from the Federal Aviation Administration documents step-by-step how-to, case studies, best practices, and lessons learned. Hooray for trash reduction being on the FAA radar (ha ha – aviation term) – more good news. Nonetheless, I still feel compelled to do my part.

I found there to be a lot of inconsistency between airlines – most support recycling with significant variations at the flight attendant level. I try to make friends with them. On another flight to somewhere in July, I told the flight attendant I did not need plastic ware to eat my $8 gourmet orzo salad in the non-recyclable plastic box (I reused it during the trip and brought it back to reuse). She tried to hand me the plastic ware a second time and I said (proudly), "No really, I don't need it, I have these!" and held up my To-Go Ware set. She was even more excited than I was, wrote down To-Go Ware's website and congratulated me for having my own utensils. This new BFF said, "Imagine if everyone did that..." Happy.

A few Flight Attendants were not pleased with my use-no-plastic efforts or didn't really seem to care. Usually when I asked them to fill my water bottle the response was neutral and I got a refill in my water bottle. Sometimes I would briefly explain/request with, "Could you put some water in here? You know, to save a cup?" Some would say, "Sure." Others would say, "I can't fill it directly but I can put it in a cup and them you can pour it into the bottle." Defeats the initial purpose – argh. Sometimes they would say, "No" and go into a long explanation about hygiene and share, "if the plane is bumpy your water bottle would touch this water bottle and which would be bad..." OK, I guess. Sometimes they acted like it was a lot more work to fill my bottle and give a little sigh while doing it. One Flight Attendant said, "I have to make sure there is enough for everyone, I can't completely fill your bottle – I can't give you more than everyone else" – OK then. I did not ask for the bottle to be filled and I am pretty sure filling my 14-ounce bottle would not deplete the water source on board. Do they think I am trying to get more water than I deserve? What is this really about? When asked about on board recycling, some Flight Attendants confidently answer yes, and some say, "We take all the trash and give it to another company and they are supposed to sort it." Whatever the policy may be is fine, just decide.

On one travel extravaganza, I was a little rushed boarding the last leg of a flight and saved my water refill for the flight. I have never been refused a refill and I had no reason to think this time would be any different. Once at cruising altitude, drinks were being served

– which by the way I NEVER need to know how high in the sky we are, thank you. I got my bottle ready and was going to deliver my standard, "Water please and could you put it in here?" while offering up the bottle to the attendant with a casual and perky, "I'm trying to save a cup!"

That wouldn't wash with Wanda, who responded, "Oh, right, uh, no." I was surprised, but complied and put my bottle away, which must have thrown her off. Perhaps she was expecting a volume argument. I figured it was a matter of time before I would be refused for sanitary reasons. If her bottle touched my bottle with unexpected turbulence it would be icky, there would be germs and it would create a very un-hygienic situation. Her bottle would become unusable and besides who knows if her bottle had touched other people's bottles. Actually, I have to agree and am willing to refill in advance. Nonetheless, Wanda felt bad for denying me – she told me she would feel responsible if I got dehydrated and offered me a plastic cup of water to pour into my bottle. It still defeats the purpose of trying to save a cup. She tried hard to give me a cup with her promise to recycle it. She even offered me the liter bottle she was pouring from! I stuck with my decision and she stuck with hers. I had to say four or five times that it was OK, I totally understood and reassured her we would be Facebook friends by the time we landed.

My positive agreement with her and her willingness to share the reasons behind her response, led us into Part One of a conversation about their policy on refilling water bottles. She wasn't sure they had one, instead she inserted her own personal policy of no refills. I respect and appreciate her airline recycling when they can. This exchange took about 5 minutes and finished with an "ahem" from the other attendant as they rolled on back to dispense more brown carbonated beverages and tomato juice and I heard "sorry" once or twice more…she truly felt bad about denying me a full water bottle filling.

Part Two of the conversation was back in the galley with

Wanda and the other two flight attendants. As I was walking back to the bathroom, I said (loud enough for W to overhear, thinking I was funny), "Wow, I am so thirsty", which served to open up the conversation again – she really did feel bad. Then I felt bad for her feeling bad. We all had a quick, deep conversation about values and sticking to them whether or not it is company policy. I explained my commitment to Recycling on the back end AND to Reducing on the front end of the 3-Rs of Reduce, Reuse, Recycle. They talked about the challenge of the inconsistent "no refill" policy between flights and even between attendants on the same flight. They had stories of unhappy, non-compliant passengers whose insistence on using their own bottles and cups made for added stress. With no policy to back them up, the reliance on their personal conviction of this seemingly easy decision to refuse a refill was admirable.

Isn't this how life is? There are no company policies to lean on or blame when it comes to personal decisions on how we live our lives, how we treat others, how we spend our time and money. Once arriving at our final destination, I said goodbye to Wanda and she said "Sorry" one more time; I replied, "It's OK, thank you," one more time and we parted ways. Lesson learned – fill early and often and be ready to back your decisions with your values – even at 32,000 feet.

A few stats to convince you to bring your own water bottle…first this from the Food and Drug Administration, "Companies promoting bottled water as being safer than tap water are defrauding the American public." The latest landfill stats for plastic water bottles being disposed of in the United States are at 30 BILLION says the Container Recycling Institute, a private 501(c)(3). Their estimate is 877 bottles wasted every second. According to Hannah Ellsbury in an article for Ban the Bottle, National Geographic says, "if we take into consideration the energy required to manufacture, transport and dispose of plastic water bottles in the United States, between 15-17 million barrels of oil (enough to fuel more than 100,000 cars for an entire year) are used each year in order to meet consumer demands. To help put things into perspective, a study performed by the Pacific Institute in California suggests bottled water production (including all stages from manufacturing the plastic to chilling the bottles for use) takes approximately 2000 times the energy required to produce tap water." Use these stats and/or choose your own credible source. Even if the actual totals are half of what is estimated by these organizations, there is room for a huge positive impact – we have control over this.

Overall, I got pretty good at eliminating plastic from my purchases with a few exceptions. I made a concession regarding my printer. My printer cartridges had #6 packaging and were not recyclable at the time. Now my county accepts plastics up to #7. The cartridges themselves can be returned to Staples for a $3 coupon – it adds up and it is good to know they are not going into the landfill! I enjoy Staples for this program and for many other reasons. My printer could not handle recycled paper for some reason – drats. Note on recycling recycled paper – according the Environmental Protection Agency (*www.epa.gov*) it is possible to recycle paper 6-7 times before the paper fibers break down so far they can no longer be recycled. So, it is still a good idea to use recycled paper and re-recycle it! I started using the Staples flipchart pads made from sugar cane. In other news, some Wegman's now have paper and compostable plastic takeout containers – good job.

On that same layover in Orlando, Mary, a dedicated teacher, had some inspiring stories and ideas for more monthly challenges. This is what usually happens when I talk about Nothing New and my no plastic month in particular. People want to share what small yet meaningful steps they are taking to preserve, reserve and conserve. She shared her ideas for a town garden – love it. She had been using plastic grocery bags in her classroom until Dan at Wegman's suggested she use the bags from the recycle bin at the store for her classroom THEN recycle. She shared clever ideas and changes she is making to teach her students responsibility for their environment. In addition, Mary did think her husband would be in favor of *her* not buying anything new.

For a convincing summary on how to look seriously at your plastic use, revisit Annie Leonard's *Story of Stuff* site and check out the *Story of Bottled Water*. This video explains how the IDEA of needing bottled water has been planted in our minds. In most instances, tap water is fine and we have been scared into believing tap water is bad. Bottled water is less sustainable, tastes worse in many cases and costs so much more. In the United States, people buy enough bottled water in a week for the bottles to circle the globe five times and, in the end, 80% of those bottles end up in the landfill or incinerator. Yikes. Bring your own bottle.

No Plastic Month was a success. Harder than I thought it would be in some ways to establish some lasting habits. I did slip three times – brought the containers back and contributed to the Nothing New Fund. You will find your own way – with both incentives and "punishments" – to help keep yourself on track. I committed to these:

- Bring my own water bottle, coffee mug, cloth napkins and To-Go Ware with me EVERYWHERE, EVERYTIME.
- Continue to reuse all my plastic zippie bags multiple times.
- Purchase more permanent containers to reduce use of zippies.
- Avoid taking plastic bags for produce at any store – don't need 'em.
- Use my reusable grocery bags at other stores – seems obvious now.
- Save egg cartons, containers and jars for Farmer's Market.
- Purchase products with less plastic packaging.

- Use more paper bags for trash – most of my wet garbage goes out to the compost bin.
- Bring my trash with me if recycling is not available.

Some quick final travel/recycle thoughts from my blog:

Day 221 – November 5, 2010 – Friday
Recycle, Recycle, Wherefore Art Thou Recycle?

I have of late, wherefore I know not, lost all my mirth, I mean plastic, OK, I mean glass. No paper! Wait, what? I have a little Shakespeare on my mind as I ponder the absence of recycling opportunities on my current trip to NE. Therefore, my suitcase is filling up with plastic, glass and paper. I even washed out the containers from Chipotle, my now FAVORITE (slow/fast food) restaurant – "local food with integrity." It is hit or miss with hotel recycling. I give huge credit to the front desk clerk for his offer to recycle the items for me. I guess there are a few individuals there recycling the stuff themselves, but why doesn't the company as whole provide it? The camp we were at did not recycle either and we were using all disposable plastic ware and Styrofoam plates. At least I had my Fab Four. I asked the students to use one cup all weekend long and put their name on it, which they did happily. Many of them had water bottles, which is good and it is frustrating to keep finding recycling to be an afterthought. Oh, they wanted me to tell you they are all turning the water off when they brush their teeth. Have a Nothing New Day!

Do what you can, whenever you can, wherever you can…

HOW TO...

1. Get your own Fab Four – use them everywhere and share your good habits and learnings with others.

2. Decide to stop buying and using plastic – no more plastic water bottles.

3. Use your purchasing power to buy only products with recyclable packaging.

4. Meet with other groups, organizations or facilities you could influence – workplace, dining hall, apartment building.

5. Commit to a list of behaviors reinforcing your beliefs about recycling.

PONDER THIS...

- What values have you had to defend?

- What organizations are you part of making it easier for you to live your values on a daily basis?

- Where/how can you best repair or repurpose before you reduce, reuse and recycle?

- What sources do you deem most credible when you are fact checking for an issue you feel strongly about?

- What changes do you want to be a part of in your organization or on your campus?

- What compels you to make a change in your life?

Detox Yourself

CLEAN AND GREEN YOUR HOME AND HEALTH

"He who wants to change the world should already begin by cleaning the dishes."

**– Paul Carvel,
Writer/editor**

The inspiration for October and November Motivation Months came from my ongoing interest in natural products. I have always been interested in this and am pretty sure I have tried most brands of every natural dish soap and hair product out there. My guidance and affirmation came from a new friend Amy Jane Stewart from Canandaigua, NY and her company Organica Jane. I am ever more educated on this front because of her. I went to one of her revealing "Home Green Home" classes in July and learned how many everyday cleaning products have pesticides in them. She has researched hundreds of products and is a smart and cool professional in the essential oils education, natural health and green living world. Her newsletter and blog offer insight on products, recalls, remedies. Check out her Organica Jane line of health products. Oh, and take a looky loo at her TV debut!

This was exactly the nudge I needed to detox my house by cleaning up my cleaning products. Did a little photo shoot with my new cleaning products. **The "before" shot included 16 products, estimated cost $53:** Dish soap, dishwasher soap and rinse aid, abrasive cleanser, laundry soap, stain pre-treat, room spray, steel wool soap pads, bleach, bleach stick, window cleaner, grease remover, wood cleaner, oven cleaner, all purpose cleaner, and toilet cleaner. **The "after" shot had 10 products estimated cost $84:** Dr. Bronner's Peppermint (magic) Soap, dishwasher soap, baking soda, Borax, Thieves Household Cleaner, vinegar, distilled water, essential oil, spray bottles, and steel wool. I now include lemon juice and salt in the After – plus sunshine and time – stain removal is a snap.

I was really interested to see how the cost/benefit piece plays out here. Some natural products are more expensive at first glance. They are concentrated to last longer and oh by the way, are better for the environment. In a nutshell, phosphates and other chemicals present in many cleansers enter our wastewater system and can become runoff affecting our streams, soil and drinking water. I found out from Kathy at Wegman's (nice, smart and very helpful) their much less expensive "Free and Clear" store brand is not tested on animals, is plant-based not made from petroleum and even though they cannot officially say the product is "all natural" it is a pretty good product. You will have to do some of your own research.

In a quick conversation the young man at the grocery checkout wanted to know why the bottle of Dr. Bronner's Soap cost $11.99. When I started to explain about chemicals and waste water and runoff, his eyes glazed over – I think he was expecting the short answer. His thought was that we don't really have to worry about the cleaning chemicals unless they somehow get out of the "system." He was pretty sure the pipes and things in the system would contain everything. I had no time to really reply and he was glad I'm sure – probably relieved to scan my last item, take my payment and send me on my way. I was still learning about this aspect of green living at the time and I was a little relieved too. Seems the main objection to natural products is cost, followed by effectiveness, then necessity. I am now able to counter all of these.

If you are looking for reasons to convert to natural cleaning products, or trying to convince a darling roommate, spouse or partner please read and share this information from NOAA (National Oceanic and Atmospheric Administration):

9/3/2010 WASHINGTON--A report issued today by key environmental and scientific federal agencies assesses the increasing prevalence of low-oxygen "dead zones" in US coastal waters and outlines a series of research and policy steps to help reverse the decades-long trend. The interagency report notes incidents of hypoxia – a condition in which oxygen levels drop so low that fish and other animals are stressed or killed – have increased nearly 30-fold since 1960. Incidents of hypoxia were documented in nearly 50 percent of the 647 waterways assessed for this report, including the Gulf of Mexico, home to one of the largest such zones in the world. [This research was done before the BP oil spill incident.] Unnatural levels of hypoxia, which occur mostly in the summer, are primarily the result of human activities delivering nutrients such as nitrogen and phosphorous into waterways. Fertilizer runoff from agricultural, urban and suburban landscapes, sewage discharges, and air pollution are major contributors. The supply of added nutrients entering bodies of water supports blooms of algae, which in turn are decomposed by oxygen-depleting bacteria. The resulting hypoxia can suffocate animals that cannot move away, such as shellfish, and – depending on how quickly the hypoxia develops – either kill or force into less suitable habitat free-swimming animals such as fish, shrimp, and crabs.

These are enough reasons for me. I like oceans, lakes, and fish. I want my nephews to inherit the clean version of these. I can decide to contribute to the problem or the solution, I choose solution. I am in. Sign me up!

Day 166 – September 11, 2010 – Saturday

A day for remembering to be sure. I remember my dad every day, this time of year more than usual. Fall was his favorite season – we did a lot of foliage day trips as a family to Kettle Moraine, Wade House, Dundee Mountain and loads of other gorgeous WI state parks (for you Cheeseheads out there). He always had a hundred questions and was uber-interested in knowing the backstory of the park staff, of the people eating their picnic lunch next to us, of the ghosts of "State Park Past." John Kenneth Skarie was a learner, a researcher, a reader, a conversationalist, a humorist, a teacher. I am sure I appreciated those trips at the time – even more so as I continue to realize who we are now as a family is because of my parents' dedication to keeping our core strong (This will relate to leaner/greener living in a second I promise). The lessons, the support, the faith and the fun all wrapped around each other and I see it in how my mom still leads us and how my brother and sister-in-law are raising their children. He reinforced many messages about safety, cleaning and general organization. Dad kept receipts, owner's manuals, newspaper articles and labeled everything. Before expiration dates were standard, he would write the purchase date on everything to make sure our refrigerator stayed safe. He believed along with the soap there needed to be some friction to actually make the item in question clean. It wasn't enough to touch the soap you had to make some movement with it. In fact, he would test us by hiding a nickel under the bar of soap in the bathroom to find out if we actually picked it up or camouflaged our sudsing activity with a splash of water from the faucet.

Last week, I spent nearly an hour one day cleaning the dish drainer pad in the kitchen sink with baking soda and

Thieves spray. During the experience, I was reminded of the importance of friction in the cleaning process. I had dreamily envisioned being able to leave the baking soda sitting there long enough by itself to remove the black "matter" accumulated in the 168 little ridges on the back of the pad. Ugh. Not the case and over the course of the day I would revisit the pad and scrub for a bit with a toothbrush – a dedicated cleaning toothbrush to clarify in case you were worried – then go away to do something else. Finally clean at the end of the day, I was able to move on from the dish drainer pad to other more important tasks.

I am not sure any cleaning product would have worked on its own as I had hoped like "set it and forget it" oven cleaner, and if it did it would most likely have some undesirable toxic elements in its DNA. The trade-off of no sweat convenience for non-toxic workout is worth it. Lesson? Good and greener cleaning takes time and effort which may end up serving as another distraction. I am the Goddess of Procrastination – ask my friends who have witnessed me polishing a silver bowl on tax day. As my laundry rotates with non-toxic laundry soap and Borax and I prepare to clean my kitchen floor with Dr. Bronner's natural soap and psyche myself up to mow my lawn with my electric mower, I could feel smug in my efforts to green my home. I know there is still more I should do AND every small significant step is a good one. Have a Nothing New Day!

Since toxic drain cleaner was out of my life for good, I was thrilled to add "natural drain-unclogging" to my skill set. Found an efficient recipe of baking soda, vinegar and hot water on The Good Human site. Satisfying to watch it work as the water drained – with only natural ingredients streaming in the waste water system. NO toxic products needed at all – safe for humans, for pets, for the environment. Hooray. Adapted their process below and jazzed it up a little. Cleaning is a joy!

Step 1 – Put ¾ Cup DRY baking soda down the drain.

Step 2 – Pour ½ Cup of vinegar down the drain after the baking soda. Be sure to cover the drain immediately afterwards with a rag or plug, filling the hole completely so nothing can escape. The interaction of the two ingredients will cause a "mini volcano" that will want to come up and out of the drain. You want to keep it down there. It is very bubbly and science-project-like.

Step 3 – Leave this concoction in the drain for about 30 minutes. While you are waiting, boil a teakettle full of water.

Step 4 – After 30 minutes, remove the plug and slowly pour the HOT water down the drain.

Step 5 – If needed, use a plunger to free up the clog. Repeat process if the drain doesn't run free.

Step 6 – Rejoice and feel proud of yourself.

I cleaned my porch chairs before putting the away for the season with all natural products. I like how my day can be made by a sparkly seating fixture. The most challenging thing about this month of "house detox" was, except for dish soap at the sinks, there is not an intense every-day-all-day feeling of habits like I had with the Local Food month. Therefore, it seemed harder to remember to NOT use the "other" products for removing label goo and the ever-so-handy bleach stick in the plastic, non-recyclable container for stains – another argh. They are quick and effective it was hard to let them go. I needed to find some good substitutes. Once I made the initial transition to buying the new products it did seem to ease up. I used up some old products first, so as not to waste what I already had. You could do it gradually – replacing old as you run out instead of buying everything at once. My learning curve was pretty steep and I was convinced what I was doing is better for everyone, everything, everywhere. As for me and my house, I am doing the best I can. If I can influence a few others with what I am doing and learning, then good!

After detoxing my house in September, I aimed to detox my beauty products in October. Starting with familiar brands, I worked hard to find ones meeting all my criteria of no animal testing, no sulfides, sulfates or other environmentally unkind ingredients, and locally made. Again, I have pretty much tried them all in some way, shape or form.

I had already settled on Aveda for the most part, where hair care and makeup was concerned. They are based in MN and the first beauty company in the world with 100% post-consumer bottles and caps, and the first beauty company manufacturing with 100% wind-generated power. I revisited a few other favorites I had used in the past and a few new ones. I really liked an organic line from Neal's Yard Remedies, made in the UK – not local at all, darn. Here is the NYR Product statement and their "just say no" list – apply this to your products to compare. Look for products with NO:

- Animal testing – unnecessary and cruel
- GMO (genetically modified organism) ingredients – not enough known about long-term implications
- Paraben – linked to estrogen overproduction
- Nano particles – not enough is known about their long-term implications
- Synthetic fragrances – often associated with allergic reactions

- Synthetic colors – often associated with allergic reactions
- Silicones – coat the skin, impeding its natural function
- Mineral oils – derived from petroleum, have a tendency to block the skin
- Phthalates – reported to have toxic impact on human and animal life
- EDTA – doesn't readily biodegrade
- Propylene glycol – derived from petroleum
- Carbomer – derived from petroleum
- DEA – associated with known carcinogens

NOTE: If you are as susceptible to clever packaging as I am, then buyer beware of "greenwashing" – attempts to avoid potential ingredient reporting or hide unpleasant or unpopular facts about a product or service. Sometimes companies claim to be green or literally make their packaging green without really implementing business practices with minimized environmental impact. Look at the Good Guide app for more insight at your point of selection in the store.

There was much excitement when I found a toothbrush made from recycled yogurt cups for $2.99 and made in the USA. A company called Preserve Products based in MA with a plant in Cortland, NY, partners with Stonyfield Yogurt in NH. It comes in a package doubling as a mailer ready with address label on the Mail Back Pack. You ship the toothbrush back to them to be recycled again when you are done. Love it. They even offer a toothbrush subscription for automatic shipment of a new toothbrush every three months – clever. They have a "Gimme #5" program to accept #5 containers that many communities do not (#1s and #2s are most common). They had me at "repurposed yogurt cup".

Big news – basic cupboard ingredients can be made into household and health products. I made a sugar scrub with mild olive oil, white sugar and a few drops of peppermint oil. Note to self (and to you) – less is more with the peppermint oil...unless you really like feeling cold for about 10 minutes after the shower – super refreshed and wide awake! Oh, and from experience, do not put the peppermint oil anywhere near your eyes. Be careful. I am still working on a natural face scrub with kitchen ingredients. Oatmeal and brown sugar are not just for breakfast anymore.

Speaking of breakfast...and soap...The Mooseberry Soap Company and Café in Fairport has soap meeting all my criteria – plus 24 beautiful and delicious scents plus hand soap, shower gel and shampoo (or "realpoo" as my dad used to say – maybe my mom too – get it? Humorous household. "Real" not a "sham" – to make it funny). Now as I continue to research Aveda, Burt's Bees and others for make-up, I use Mary's products almost exclusively for skin care. A real find. She is a talented chef too – I recommend the "Compost Plate" as an alternative to the Made-Famous-In-Rochester Garbage Plate.

If October was Use No Hot Water Month, I would have won a prize! My water heater was DONE (it was 21 years old) and I had to buy a new one. Gratefully, I have a network of people who know people who know people and I was able to find a competitive price on the heater. It was installed by friends in exchange for fermented malt beverages – thank you again Joe. Not an amusing expenditure but allowed me to celebrate Pioneer Days on Monroe Street while waiting days for the new water heater. My "showers" only required two pots of hot, hot water, diluted with some cold – it was more than enough. I'm sure I was using too much water – I do already pay attention and turn the faucet off during teeth brushing. Good for me and as I have learned in prior months, I am sure I can do more.

I wish you luck if you are on a journey to detoxing yourself and your house/apartment/room with natural products. My main advice is do the research and stick to whatever criteria you set for yourself and your household. Your habits will take root in a short time and in the long run you will feel good about how you are cleaning and greening! Besides the structure you live in, your most important house is your body....

HOW TO...

1. Determine your ingredient "must have/must not have" criteria for your products.

2. Educate yourself on the ingredients in your favorite products and research any claims and results.

3. Switch to greener products that make sense for you and affirm your "why".

4. Track the money you spend/save over time and confirm if it is worth it.

5. Be prepared to explain your decisions/choices and allow time for yourself and others to adjust.

PONDER THIS...

- What are your go-to brands for cleaning and health/beauty care products and why?

- Are you confident the products you buy and use reflect your values?

- What style of packaging really pulls you in and compels you to buy a product?

- Are there certain smells/scents indicating "clean" to you if absent would require a shift in thinking?

- Who would benefit from a change in cleaning and hygiene products in your family/living group?

- Remember to remember the small, significant things... what do you have, who do you love, who you miss and why do you what you do?

Make Stuff

There's a Little Bit of Love (and Cat Hair) in Everything Handmade

"To be rich in admiration and free from envy, to rejoice greatly in the good of others, to love with such generosity of heart that your love is still a dear possession in absence or unkindness – these are the gifts which money cannot buy."

**– Robert Louis Stevenson,
Author (1850-1894)**

As a much younger version of myself, I learned to sew because my mom sewed and her mom sewed. I aced Home Ec with my final sundress project and recall my first batch of chocolate chip cookies turning out quite nicely. I continued to enjoy these things as an adult. In my Year of Nothing New, this skill set was revisited and refined, not to the point of having my own HGTV show, enough to contribute a pin or two on Pinterest!

Growing up, my Marcia made stuff. I still have two baby cardigan sweaters she made for me and I pull out her handcrafted ornaments each Christmas. She made dolls, doll clothes, puppets, hats and pillows. She sewed a lot of clothes for me too. There was always a cute outfit for Easter and Christmas, first day of school and a party dress or two. I recall a red velvet dress with a white satiny part and a bow on top, plaid skirts, shorts and halter-tops. I still have the dance recital costumes she made – I am pretty sure those costumes were a "1" on the fun scale, 1 being very low. She knit, crocheted and macramé-ed her way through the 60s and 70s which kept me in high fashion all the way through Junior High – a rainbow (crocheted) vest, pink striped pantsuit and animal print jumper put me way ahead of the curve. She made stuff. Oh, and she was an expert at rosemaling (Norwegian decorative painting) – she indeed made stuff.

My mom's mom made stuff. I'm pretty sure each of us 11 grandkids has a knit afghan from her. Every year she made each one of the five granddaughters a flannel nightgown with a tag inside inside reading, "Specially Handmade by Grandma." Most times, I would go with her to the fabric store to pick out a new favorite. One of the best handmade presents I have ever been given is a quilt with patches of flannel from all the nightgowns Grandma had made me over the years. She made mittens for needy kids, crafts for the elderly and plastic canvas goodies to be sold in the gift shop of her retirement center until she was 95. She made stuff.

I strive to make stuff with a range of success. Which brings me to the Fourth Question people would ask after 1) food, 2) why, 3) shampoo: "Did you buy new stuff for people or did you make stuff?" I'm glad you asked!

My commitment this year was to give either secondhand items or use secondhand items to make the gifts. I started out strong with good intentions. I had been stocking up on used picture frames with the idea of framing some photos I had taken on my trips – shamrocks in the forests of California, aspen trees in Colorado, and swimming star nephews in Florida. Then most of the frames did not really go with the photos, so I bought new frames. I also framed some (new) unusual square greeting cards (new) with quotes on them. Grr.

Therefore, I decided to the best of my abilities, I would make *something* even if I had to buy new materials, there would be some element of "Specially Handmade by Kristin." Given the fact I started most of the gifting preparation process on December 10 for the Christmas holiday season, this was my best effort. I allowed the purchase of consumables/experiences like restaurants, movies or carwashes as a present in and of itself or to supplement these handmade gifts. See more on "what is enough" later...

Most of my friends and family appreciate something handmade – I have a few friends who do not. I know this and it's OK. I made some strategic decisions about what to make and for whom. Here's a sample:

- Lavender body oil and lavender sugar scrub stored in glass jars and bottles
- Spicy walnuts in paper bags – lunch sacks with my hand stamped greeting on front
- Cranberry-walnut chutney in glass jars
- Blue and white soap dish for Mom (second hand) – her kitchen is blue and yellow
- Peppermint bark and hot chocolate (my favorite brand packaging says, "buy me" – I have the recipe now and will make be making this in 2013)
- Candles in glass vases with little green stones (had them) – super decorative if I may say
- Chocolate oranges – a tradition for Casey and Cobi
- Book for Olivia (new – she was 3 and would not understand the whole used/handmade thing…or did I sell her short?)
- Wooden toy logs to make a mini log cabin for JoeyO – he was in the process of building a real log cabin and all he wanted for Christmas was a log cabin. I delivered.

I defaulted to gift cards for some friends because it seemed like a gray area. Is it? Bookstore, iTunes, coffee shop are somewhat consumable. Are they? I went way outside the lines with beautiful wall tiles (handmade in New Zealand) from a shop in Rochester called Old House Parts – maybe I get points for buying local. Rounded out the season and ordered Ugly Dolls for my nephews which are unattractive, loveable, stuffed toys. If you are an uncle or auntie you know what it is like to want to spoil the children. I do wonder if I underestimated their ability to understand what I was doing. They probably would have liked a trip to the movies or water park as their gift. To my amazement, the Ugly Dolls were pretty sweet and still have a spot on my nephews' beds to this day.

I am proud I did not completely give in to materialism that giving season...the fact I resisted buying a Presidential Sprouting Seed Head for Sue Mahon says a lot about my discipline and tenacity. Someone else gave her one and I got to see what it looked like. All told, I spent $321 on new items to make stuff for 19 people, about $17 per person, and added the new total to my Nothing New Fund. Once the holidays were over I gave myself a C+ for not really sticking to my original plan. Nonetheless, I felt good about my endeavor and made plans for 2011 to try again with the handmade things.

I gave other presents – a few thank you's and a scattering of presents for birthdays and anniversaries. A small silver box of See's Chocolates from their headquarter city of San Francisco to thank Hannah for kitty sitting was a hit as an instant cure to an after-school snack attack. My dad used to bring See's Candy for us when he traveled which made me feel like there was a story behind the candy. Meaningful (consumable) gift with a back story – a good thing. Got to see H model her prom dress – a long, gorgeous eggplant-colored gown – a quarter of the full retail price at a consignment shop – tags still on. Go Hannah. I have known her since she was 8 years old and she has always had a knack for "greener" shopping.

Do you remember what you received from every person who gave you a gift for your last birthday or significant holiday? It's OK if you don't. I think most of us don't remember and I include myself in this. I am sure there is joy for the giver and receiver of the gift at the time. And for some people and some gifts I suppose there is a longer lasting or more significant memory. I think the same is true for souvenirs. I got in better habits this year of bringing the memories, the photos, the gratitude and the learnings as gifts to myself and for others – leaving the stuff behind. On the same trip to Utah when I met up with Gina and her To-Go Ware, I had a chance to go out to Park City to scout out a souvenir…

Day 62 – May 19, 2010 – Wednesday

Looked around the FREE Park City History Museum first, checked out a few consignment shops and saw mostly rows of colorful cowboy boots – hmmm. Wanted to grab lunch at Robert Redford's restaurant "Zoom" – he had of course invited me – it was closed for lunch during the "shoulder" season. I understood the shoulder season concept as the time between winter and summer. The shoulder of a road is between the high part and the low/steep part, or it's the part between the neck and the arm on the body, or bottles have shoulders where the neck expands out to the body, resembling a human shoulder. Learning. Always learning. Have a Nothing New Day!

The best souvenir or gift for myself has a story – or is the story in itself. The best souvenir for someone else includes them in the experience you have had – something personal, unique, memorable, sentimental or beautiful. I didn't find anything to bring back from the Utah trip – instead I met some people, saw the sights, and learned a lot. The idea of a souvenir as a THING demonstrating proof of an experience is perhaps too narrow a definition. Isn't the experience itself enough? As a traveler, these and other questions roll around my mind all the time. Ah, years that ask questions…

One year as a gift, I compiled over 10 years worth of letters and emails my dad had sent me into a document cleverly entitled, "Letters from Dad," for my mom and my brother, Erik. They liked it – they really liked it. I have felt good about giving local peaches as a seasonal tradition (juice dripping down your elbows), a laminated collage of cut-out magazine images, a family cross-stitch, a framed wedding program, an antique coffee tin and a small box with a mysterious key inside and the Shakespeare quote "Tis in my memory locked. And you yourself shall keep the key of it." I have both given and received the treasured gift of a place to live for a while, a listening ear and friendship. There is no guarantee the receivers feel the same as you do in a gift exchange. Seems trite, but what if one year all you did was exchange friendship and that was enough? Memorable gifts received? So many...

What is enough? Is WHAT you are giving as a gift enough? Or are you really thinking about if YOU are enough? It has definitely been the case for me in the past. Do the handmade candle-holders given match the beautiful 100-inch strand of pearls received? Does it matter? I do believe it is the thought that counts. Shrug of shoulders. My default settings are to offer any gift with humility and to receive every gift with grace. Maybe it all comes down to the meaning we attach to the object, the experience and the relationship.

A final thought attributed to the National Trust, a British historic preservation society reads, "Tread lightly, take only pictures, leave only footprints, kill only time." And make some stuff.

HOW TO...

1. Set your parameters – hand made, second hand only? Useable, consumable, reusable...?

2. Figure out what skills/tools/facilities/resources you have access to in order to make something (and would enjoy making!).

3. Tailor your handmade gifts for each person as you would any other gift.

4. Set a budget and timeline for the completed item(s) – and start way earlier than you think you should.

5. Be prepared for a range of reactions to your handmade treasure – know in your heart you made it with care.

BONUS: Regarding souvenirs, make a budget/ purchasing decision in advance as to who you will buy for and remember – stories are souvenirs.

PONDER THIS...

- Are you a stuff maker? Why or why not?

- What is the best gift anyone ever made for you (or gave you) and why?

- What gift have you made for (or given to) someone else that was well received and why?

- What traditions do you have for gift giving and where did they originate?

- How have you handled an unequal or awkward gifting situation?

- When are the times you feel like YOU are enough? With whom? Why?

Clean Your Closet

Ten Black Cardigans

"If most of us are ashamed of shabby clothes and shoddy furniture, let us be more ashamed of shabby ideas and shoddy philosophies...It would be a sad situation if the wrapper were better than the meat wrapped inside it."

– Albert Einstein,
Physicist (1879-1955)

I may have to blame Mom and she knows this. It all started with her "Specially Handmade by Marcia" baby cardigans. It brought me to a place of overabundance in the clothing area and for as long as I can remember I have had a definite interest in clothes. In sixth grade, I am sure I was the first to wear a midi-length vest over a mini-skirt, not to be confused with a midi-skirt or maxi-skirt – the 70s were complicated. Marcia-made, it was thin wale corduroy in a red, white and blue circle-y print with a blue lining. I remember walking down the hallway in school, a little uncomfortable because no one else was wearing what I was wearing, and at the same time thinking, "I am cool." Channeling my inner Peggy Lipton from The Mod Squad got me through the day. She was cool and I am sure she had a midi-vest.

Flash forward almost 40 years later and I still love clothes – remember I banned myself from the mall for Nothing New? In 2010, I had two closets full of clothes and a few too many cardigans. 10 of them were black. Mind you they were all a bit different – long sleeve, ¾ sleeve, V-neck, crew neck, ruffles, flowers, some longer, some shorter, snaps, buttons – I could go on. Will name my next cat, Cardigan.

With the help of my teenaged friend, Michaela Brew, we took 2 hours and went through my closet item by item. She let me keep five black cardigans – a regular classic crew neck, a longer one with snaps, a ¾ sleeve with ruffles, one with beading and one with ruffles AND a zipper. I tried to keep a very 90s pink satin-lined, black velvet zip hoodie to no avail. I am pretty sure the word Michaela used to describe this item was "appalling." In the end, I had two bags of clothing for consignment.

The closet cleaning was a continuation of my quest to de-clutter launched the month before when I decided to finally clean my office to find all my craft stuff. Best tool for this whole process was the blog of a woman who calls herself the Unclutterer. Erin Rooney Doland shares daily tips for reducing clutter – about staying organized with the "place for everything, and everything in its place" philosophy. Papers, kid's artwork, laundry, technology, junk drawers, finances, garage, moving, pets, storage – everything! Her Uni-tasker Wednesday posts highlight single use items we should NEVER buy such as the Egg and Spoon Race Set, Stick Pet Toy, and the French Fry Holder for your car. Her blog will be your ultimate source for more of these items and what NOT to buy. I implemented one of Erin's ideas my friend Shelby set up in her house – a Donation Station. This is a single spot where I immediately place and store items for donation in 4 separate bags, 1) Vietnam Vets (clothing and household – they will come to you for pick up), 2) Craft Bits & Pieces (crafts and knick knacks), 3) Farmers Market (produce/egg containers) and 4) Anything Goes (consignment).

On this theme, my January Motivation month would involve a Fashion Fast as described by Eric Wilson in his New York Times Style Magazine article. The people he interviewed wore only six items of clothing for one month (excluding undergarments, shoes and accessories) and learned some really meaningful things...I marinated in this idea for a week and came up with my list of what to wear for January 9-February 9:

1 Blazer (gray/black)
1 Pair of jeans (dark/dressy)
1 White dress shirt
1 Sweater dress (long black)
1 Long sleeve T-shirt (black)
1 V-neck sweater (black)

I allowed PJ's, one workout outfit and two coats (a dress coat and a super warm casual jacket – it is after all winter in Rochester). I accessorized freely – scarves, clip-on flowers and jewelry. This was challenging in the beginning then easy as I got into the groove. Like the NY Times "Fashion Fast-inistas," people never really noticed or seemed not to care if they did. OK then. I did add one item of clothing for a few hours on the 2011 Superbowl Sunday – my one and only good luck Green Bay Packers T-shirt! The Packers beat the Steelers 31-25.

A few clothing stats: Week 1 – I stuck to the 6 items of clothing – good! Week 2 – still on board with the 6 items of clothing, then replaced black cardigan with a long black sweater and white shirt with a long black short sleeve floaty top with a satin band at the bottom. Now a confession – I wore a dressy suit for four hours at an awards luncheon. I had forgotten about the event and even my nice jeans would not have been appropriate. This limited clothing thing was easy in some ways for making packing decisions and was a little more challenging than I thought in choosing the right items. The black cardigan was not warm enough for day-to-day wear. I don't really even like that black cardigan and, in fact, "released it" to the consignment pile. I do quite like the long black cowl neck sweater and the black floaty top and felt good about the switch. I did not start the month over though. Even in such a short time, I daydreamed about the bright pink cardigan living in the back of the closet and became highly appreciative (more than usual) of a closet full of clothes. At the end of the month, I went through everything leaving only the items I love. It was clarifying and freeing!

It took me about 20 minutes to figure out what to wear on February 10 when the Fashion Fast was over. I was out of practice in making clothing decisions and the stuff in my closet seemed foreign to me. I did select the bright pink cardigan the day my Fashion Fast was over which was a welcome change from all the black I had been wearing. Overall it was such a good experience, so I replicated the Fashion Fast at a conference in Louisville, KY in March 2012 with my friend Karen Myers to raise awareness and funding for Dress for Success – good times.

As I was telling a friend about my Nothing New endeavor and Fashion Fast, I was once again reminded of the privilege I have to be able to implement this experience. Along with learning about Ted Williams that week – the homeless man with The Golden Voice in Columbus, OH – I knew how blessed I was to have what I have.

If you decide to do a Fashion Fast, my suggestions to you are:

1. Pick the right month – note all out of the ordinary events and choose the clothing items appropriate for everything – unless you want to allow some exceptions – you make the rules!
2. I know only 6 items seems extreme – I wanted to stay as close as possible to the NY Times experiment as possible. The trade-off of variety for freedom from decision-making was very refreshing.
3. Pick comfortable items you wear frequently.
4. Select items you can wear together in any combination.
5. Neutral colors rule. I chose black – my fav color to wear because it's easy and unnoticeable for the most part and goes with everything.

6. Be open to combine and accessorize...the long-sleeve black shirt can be worn under the short sleeve floaty thing under the jacket – WITH A BELT. Yes, I am a Fashion Risk-Taker.

And now a word from our local blogger:

DAY 287 – January 10, 2011 – Monday
Baby, It's Cold Inside

Hello – I decided to save my clean clothes items for my pending trip to avoid doing laundry and opted for the workout/painting outfit today. Hopes of placing some "Atmospheric Blue" onto the walls of my bedroom. Only got as far as finishing up the prep taping. Maybe tomorrow. These additional costume changes are somewhat beyond the whole Six Items Thing. I am the one making the rules after all with the main point being to see what I really NEED to have in terms of a public wardrobe. You will make your own rules. News flash: Packed in 15 minutes – easy peasy, lemon squeezy. A tiny little miracle, really. This trip will be the first real test of the 6 items – will tell all – not sure if this would have been easier in a warmer month...I sure know how to live it up. Easily amused. Will add coat and gloves to my suitcase later although I may put on the hat right now – it is chilly in here. The bones of my house are cold. She told me today as I added a little more clear tape to the edges of her plastic-dressed windows. My bones were cold today. I layered as much as I could – added a scarf to the outfit. My office window faces north and my desk is as near to the natural light as possible. A creative little breeze comes out of the closet to my left if I do not close the door (curtain). I was in good company with the indoor/outdoor attire – was informed on a call with Amy Shaffer today – she wore her wool hat all day inside. Fashion sacrifice for comfort. Off to finish some handouts. Have a Nothing New Day and stay warm!

The next morning, I woke up to a brisk 53 degree house. I knew something was not quite right the day before when it seemed chilly. I only had to endure a few hours of cold until the furnace man fixed things right up for $337. Had to buy a new ignitor – a ceramic and metal thingy the size of a large spool of thread. Until now, the word ignitor was not in my general vocabulary. Thankful for my house and the means to keep it warm.

Went into the public realm in a combo workout/pj situation (mail, bank, doc) to save the clean clothes for my next trip. I am certain there are some rules about going "out there" and I wanted to be sure and adhere to basic societal standards. On the other hand, does it really matter what one wears? Clean – yes, it is best. Good coverage – for sure yes. Age appropriate – mostly yes. In "style" (what does in style really mean) – no.

I can remember Erik offering Mom some unsolicited advice on the coolness factor of a white visor she was sporting at the time. Apparently not fond of visors (nothing against visors) he told her, "Once you're 50, you probably won't care what other people think about what you wear." I think there is some truth and freedom in there. Thanks Brother! Wear what you love even if you have it in every color. All of us have a uniform of sorts I suppose – I sort of like that.

On April 8, 2010, Day 21 of my Year of Nothing New, I shared my experiment in public for the first time with over 400 students and staff at a National Conference on Student Leadership in Atlanta. Significant timing, the habits of not shopping should have been set by then but I was still working on it. Nonetheless, they affirmed my endeavors and I was pleasantly surprised by people thinking this whole thing was a good idea. I shared a bit of the back story and a few of my pending Motivation Months. I was wearing a favorite item of clothing and one woman said, "I am glad you bought the cute white jacket you're wearing before you started this." Nice!

At the time of writing this, I am working out of one very tidy closet with very few new items. This month helped me realign this aspect of my somewhat cluttered life and set the stage to do the same in other areas. I still enjoy clothes – with a tempered wallet and a reasonable budget. The mall no longer interests me, in fact I continue to make solid efforts to avoid it except for picking up my contact lenses. A quieting and redefining month.

I clothe myself "with compassion, kindness, humility, gentleness and patience" (Colossians 3:12, NIV).

HOW TO...

1. Ask a brutally honest friend to help you clean out your closet(s) and help you as seen on "What Not to Wear."

2. Set a timeframe for the clean up/clean out.

3. Use a "20 Minutes at a Time Method" (thanks Mom) to keep your closet/living space uncluttered. Set the timer and marvel at what you accomplish.

4. Find the donation/consignment shops in your area.

5. Set up a Donation Station somewhere in your living space.

6. Release items you no longer want for someone else to enjoy...

PONDER THIS...

- What were the messages you got growing up around clothing/fashion?

- Do you have a clothing/attire/shopping downfall? If so, what is it? Sunglasses, watches, shoes, purses, cardigans?

- What is your "uniform" – your signature style or clothing items?

- Besides actual clothing, what do you "wear" every day (attitude, values, behaviors) giving others a sense of who you are?

- How could you use a Fashion Fast as a fundraiser in your community, your campus, or in your organization?

- What might you need to free yourself from?

Track Your Trash

AWAY JUST MEANS AWAY FROM YOU

"Water and air, the two essential fluids on which all life depends, have become global garbage cans."

**– Jacques Cousteau,
Explorer (1910-1997)**

The month of February allowed me to take a serious look at how much trash I created and to work hard to reduce it. Even though I composted and recycled, I knew I could do better. The average person in the US creates 4.3 pounds of garbage a day according to the Duke University Center for Sustainability and Commerce. Almost the size of a bag of sugar. Picture 30 of those bags of sugar as your trash contribution to the landfills each month. Not OK. I wanted to buck this trend in my life and stop contributing in this way! By paying more attention to packaging in particular, I ended up reducing my trash creation from four bags a month to three. I was recycling more judiciously which increased what I was recycling from two bags to three bags a month. At least I was creating less trash. I have a garbage disposal and it took me while to release the habit of putting things down the drain and use the three-step compost system I had set up. I had composted before at various camps and was familiar and interested in making this work.

1. Place scraps into repurposed large Chobani container under the sink
2. Take out to the 10 gallon bucket on the back porch
3. Bring out back to the compost bin

Compost first, recycle second, trash third. Much can be composted and I am amazed at how it all works out there in my compost pile – even on the coldest day. I dumped a bucket of biodegradable yumminess out there about once a week. Every time I went out to make a deposit, the pile was back down to where it was the week before – gotta love nature. I felt good about this AND I was concerned how composting was becoming a bright spot it my life, hey, whatever it takes right? Check out this website to join the thousands of happy, peppy people who compost – *www.howtocompost.org*. No animal products allowed (meat or dairy), but food scraps, coffee grounds, grass clippings, leaves, dryer lint, newspaper, paper bags and eggshells are OK. If you are really serious about using the compost in your garden – eggshells can contain salmonella so it may be best to trash those. PS. I added worms to my compost in Year Two…they didn't make it…Update in 2013 – like magic, the worms are in there again – welcome back!

I got carried away at one point with the compostable Sun Chip bags – people thought they were too loud, remember? I had a bit of a rant in my blog. I have toned it down a little here. I hope it speaks to how, in my opinion, priorities can get mixed up.

DAY 230 – November 14, 2010 – Sunday
Really? A Rant on Sun Chip Bag Dislikers

I found out the revolutionary, biodegradable, compostable Sun Chip bag is going to be discontinued in the US because the bag is too loud. Really? Too loud for what? Take them out of the bag and put them in a bowl. Too loud? Stop trying to sneak a handful of chips in the middle of the night. Too loud? Rise off the couch and stop watching NOTHING on TV. Too loud? Deal with it because it reduces waste and the product tastes great. This must mean there are people out there with enough free time to complain in general about a chip bag – enough time to complain to Frito-Lay and enough time create a Facebook page to complain. 53,249 people like the "SORRY BUT I CAN'T HEAR YOU OVER THIS SUN CHIPS BAG" page. Really? My message to the 53,249: Care more about the environment and work on bigger issues than loud snack bags. I really hope Frito-Lay reverses their decision and continues producing the bag here. Do not cave to misguided and narrow-minded consumers FL! To be fair, I can see the business side of FL's decision, there was an 11% decrease in sales of chips in the new bag over the past year. Shame on us as consumers then. I am personally bummed – in a "non-life threatening/I will be able to move on by tomorrow" kind of way. I had been buying only Sun Chips in the compostable bag for every snack need – even when I REALLY wanted potato chips with my sandwich or tortilla chips with my salsa. I know, I know, should be eating carrots. Fast Company Magazine had a little article on this by Ariel Schwartz – check it out. I will continue to buy Sun Chips – their plant in Modesto, CA – 1 of 8 plants – uses solar energy to create the chips there. I am going to have a little snack now – plug your ears. Have a Nothing New Day!

The loud bags are still made in Canada – they offer earplugs. Now back to trash. Happily, my town provides weekly recycling pick up and collects my large clear trash bags of paper, glass and aluminum. I appreciate this and am glad to have recycling in my habit skill set and as a service. Most of the recycle bag is filled with paper. Paper, so much paper. Junk mail, catalogs, newsletters, promotions, on and on – I called and got off the mailing lists any time I could. Envelopes with annoying cellophane windows I removed and threw away dominated the paper mix along with juice bottles, cat food cans, laundry soap bottles and other grocery related containers. I have since discovered the Paper Karma app, which takes your scanned address image and contacts the company sending you the mail. Between those two actions, I pretty much reduced the junk mail I receive to zero. Seems to be good for at least 6 months – some of the mailings started up again after a while. I realized besides reducing my trash, I had a lot of room for reducing the amount of stuff I recycle! I moved to local apple cider and grape juice in glass bottles instead of non-local OJ in plastic. I cut back on the canned cat food. Must discuss any other pending canned cat food changes with my cats.

Decided to give up brown carbonated beverages (BCB) for the month – not only was it totally inconsistent with my other eat local/ buy local habits I was infusing into my life, it made no sense from a trash standpoint. Yes the paper box is recyclable and the cans go back for deposit to be recycled, it still made no sense. The whole point was to Reduce first, duh. By Day 7 with no BCB it seemed my sugar cravings had subsided, which is a good thing. My potato chip craving did not. I have no discipline. I cut those out too for this month. Really. Until March 19, 2011. For real. Had to make some tough decisions at Wegman's – to buy locally grown greenhouse lettuce in a #5 container (not recyclable at the time) or lettuce from CA in a little plastic bag I can use again or recycle. I opted for the CA lettuce – now I am thinking I should have gone with the local lettuce and found a re-use for the silly container. What do you think?

HOW TO...

1. Compost if you can! Or lobby to have your campus, workplace, or apartment complex to set it up.

2. Track your personal trash creation for a day by carrying it all with you – is it about 5 pounds?

3. Track your trash for one month and work to decrease it each month following...invite friends to join you and make a contest out of it in your workplace or on your campus.

4. Look at your trash habits trash and pick one (or all) of them to address.

5. Visit a landfill.

PONDER THIS...

- What do you care so passionately about it would cause you to "rant?"

- Where might there be inconsistencies between what you believe and what you do?

- How do you make decisions when it is "right vs. right" e.g. local lettuce vs. recyclable container?

- Do you consider yourself an activist? Why or why not?

- If you had unlimited time, what environmental/ economic (or other) issue would prompt you to be an activist?

- What can you do starting today to create less trash?

Guzzle Less Gas
ANOTHER ONE (ALMOST) RIDES THE BUS

"Do not let what you cannot do interfere with what you can do."

**– John Wooden,
US basketball player and coach (1910-2010)**

I had decided my final challenge was to be around reduced use of my car. I tracked gas purchase and miles and it was rewarding to see a difference in what I spent. Hard to do a monthly and year-to-year comparison because it depended on where my work took me. The destinations are not set or on a regular schedule. Nonetheless, it is an area with huge impact potential and much of it is within my control.

Because I travel for work long distances – flying and driving – my carbon footprint is very large – Sasquatch-sized. How I drive, live and fly creates a carbon footprint triple threat. A carbon footprint calculator estimates how many tons of carbon dioxide and other greenhouse gases our choices create each year. It takes information you share about your lifestyle behaviors and crunches the numbers to result in your customized CO_2 number. Utilities use, air/car travel, number of cars owned, what you eat, fashion, packaging, furniture/electronic purchases, recycling, recreation and use of banking/financial institutions are all factored into your score. Check out the website *www.carbonfootprint.com* for a little reality check. This site offers suggestions on how to reduce your impact – many of these are pretty extreme for most people. What if you picked one? Or did a version of another? Or did your best in all of them?

- Buy used clothes
- Be vegan
- Recycle or compost everything
- Eat only local/seasonal food
- Grow all your own
- Participate in activities with a smaller carbon footprint – bike/walk instead of eating out/going to the movies
- Get rid of your car

In spite of my efforts to reduce in many areas of my life, I produce over **34** metric tons of CO_2 a year. Nice. Not what I was expecting. My efforts were good at a micro level however, I had not been thinking about the big-ticket items in my consumer life – driving, flying, and utilities. Some stats on carbon footprint according to this site – I produce over 3 times more CO_2 than the average person in an industrial nation...awesome. Here is some data:

- The average footprint for people in United States is 20 metric tons
- The average for people in industrial nations is about 11 metric tons
- The average worldwide carbon footprint per person is about 4 metric tons
- The worldwide target to combat climate change is 2 metric tons

I reentered my information for 2013 and I have improved. *"Your footprint is **13.59** metric tons per year."* This is encouraging! I attribute it to flying a lot less, significant changes in my eating, buying secondhand clothing and recycling. Small things do make a difference and I still have a lot of work to do.

The idea of Reducing My Fat Footprint Month compelled me to do my research on how to ride the bus in Rochester. It would involve one transfer downtown and an hour and a half to travel a total of nine miles – usually a fifteen to twenty minute drive. I still envisioned myself taking the bus to my volunteer gig at Henry Hudson School 28 – I was going about once a week and it seemed like a good, contained, reasonable and challenging goal. This entry from my blog:

Day 322 – February 14, 2011 – Monday

Even the best-laid plans do not play out the way we envision…My "ride the bus" month did not happen – at all. I could not quite make the time to track the schedule, find the stops and build in the buffer travel time. I plan to table this challenge for my second year of Nothing New. I have decided to stay on this track for another year, implement all my learning's from this year and apply them on a new level in Year Two. More to follow on my plans for ramping things up for Part Duex. Have a Nothing New Day!

Fail. Notice how I breezed over the misstep and chirped on merrily about Year Two. Bummer. I had it all mapped out, made a folder labeled BUS and even called to make sure I had the right route. My excuses were – I am busy, self-employed, and I am already volunteering 5 hours a week including prep time. Disappointing still. I have such an easy life what with a working car, a valid driver's license and a good driving record (except for a bit of speeding trouble in PA years ago – it is taken care of I promise). I have total freedom to go anywhere anytime. My car is like a little apartment on wheels containing a small wardrobe, substantial snacks and water supply, a tent and a sleeping bag in case of emergency.

It took me a while to forgive myself on this one – I felt guilty for not following through. I did commit to 2 "no drive days" a week, planned all my errands on the most efficient route and began a process still in the works to fly less for work. I flew 10 times in 2010 – 24,450 miles with a CO_2 use of 3.88 metric tons. Kristin Skarie – High Impact Girl. Not the Super Hero name I would have chosen for myself!

Here is some snapshot data on my gas/fuel use from the Nothing New Year March 2010-11 and Year 2, March 2011-12. There are a few variables making it hard to do an accurate comparison. Peruse this in your free time whilst enjoying a local, seasonal meal…

	Nothing New:	Year 2:	Difference:
Gas	$2515	$3563	$1048 increase
Air travel	$2967	$1409	$1558 decrease
Total	**$5482**	**$4972**	**$510 net decrease**

HOW TO...

1. Determine your carbon footprint.

2. Set a goal for infusing carbon-footprint-reducing behavior into your daily living.

3. Harness the power your numbers – know exactly what you spend on transportation.

4. Gather groups for biking, walking, cooking and other activities with a lower footprint.

5. Live in the "judgment-free zone" when others do what you perceive to be "less" in reducing their negative impact on the planet.

PONDER THIS...

- How do you handle failure?

- What one thing can you do to reduce your gas/fuel consumption starting today?

- Where or with whom can you share a ride?

- What awareness levels can you raise in your organization, campus or workplace around gas and fuel consumption?

- What freedoms do you have and how do you value them?

- Why is your bike sitting in the garage with a flat tire?

Leadership Lessons
HMMM'S AND AHA'S

"Did you learn anything?"

– John K. Skarie,
My Father (1928-1997)

He would usually ask us this easy question after my brother or I had done something dumb. It was asked with the emphasis on LEARN and with the assumption something was indeed learned. The answer needed to be yes and we would be prompted from there to explain even though Dad already knew what the lesson was and what he wanted us to learn. If he were around today, this would have been his first question to me about my Year of Nothing New.

Did I learn anything? Yes. More is not always better. Peace of mind comes from living my values. Me living my values can be a model for others. My habits define my success. Giving my all – all the time – and being left with nothing much of the time is exhausting. I can extend my shelf life with careful use of my time. I am enough.

A few more lessons learned here. As you turn them over in your mental compost, would you wonder about which ones might apply to you? I offer these as wishes to carry with you on your life voyage. I share them in Twitter form here because I was feeling creative. Follow along on @nothingnewchallenge and @Lead_Green. Someday, I hope you and I can sit at a local coffee shop to swap stories in person – I'll buy. @kristinskarie

An issue you "rant" about defines what you care about
#sunchipbaglovers

Personal energy is a commodity **#leadgreen**

Control over your quality of health is possible
#giveupsoda

Giving back and paying forward are their own rewards
#servantleader

Saying no (thank you) is empowering **#boundaries**

If something is important enough you will make the time
#useyour24

Just keep swimming, just keep swimming
#doryhaditright

Less is less and that is more **#yes**

Food comes from farms **#notthegrocerystore**

Money saved is time earned **#ificouldsavetimeinabottle**

Some friendships have a shelf life **#expired**

Some friendships are not **#pleaseleavenow**

Define how to give 100% to something **#allin #fearless**

Naysayers are either afraid, confused, or jealous – be kind
to them **#gracious**

Release what does not fill you **#letitgo**

Release bad influences **#lifeisshort**

Release bad shoes **#lifeislong**

Everyone is doing the best they can with the tools they have at the time **#momwisdom**

Treasure your food, clothing and shelter **#enough**

Values = priorities creates personal world peace **#passiton**

Have, Need, Want in that order not Want, Need, Have **#congruence**

You are enough **#perfect #asis**

The most significant outcomes of *A Year of Nothing New*? I ended eight work/service commitments in Year Two. My plate had grown to overflowing in 2009 and 2010 with things for which I had lost interest, felt like was no longer a contributor or there was a values mismatch. Some of them were up for renewal and I let them go. I passed a writing project on to my friend Julie Beck and felt really good about it. It was hard to release a few of the other commitments because they were positive and I really enjoyed the people.

Second, the free space on my plate left room for other things in the years following. I was careful to not slide back to overflowing. I had room to become more deeply involved with my volunteer work as a Pencil Partner with elementary school kids in our city schools. The trending of less-is-better left room for bringing two wonderful college student interns into Teamworks, Christina Bakos and David Dodge. They are my mentors and friends. There was time to write an academic article, finish this book and to be more involved on the ACPA Foundation Board (American College Personnel Association). I believe the blank spaces on my plate allowed me to be open for a position on Semester at Sea next summer – and I thought I was done traveling.

Third, the values realignment is shifting me toward the creation of more time for family and friends. I recall another breakthrough New Year's Revelation back in the 90s, which caused me to paint my bedroom ceiling with blue sky, clouds and glow-in-the-dark stars. A series of unfortunate events forced me to I boil down my priorities to 6Fs – Faith, Family, Friends, Finance, Fitness, Fun. I once again returned to my own basics.

As I sit here in over-caffeinated, peri-menopausal wonder at how the past four years have slid by, it is time to wrap this up. We are heading into fall up here in the north and it is always bittersweet. Even with the chaos of August and the fresh beginnings of new school shoes it brings quiet endings. What is the life metaphor for picking the last lettuce of the season, mowing for the last time, putting the porch stuff away, cleaning up the yard and getting the mittens out? The rituals of closing down are comforting and familiar. And in so many ways, Nothing New.

Nothing New Challenge
TAKE ACTION!

"We need much less than we think we need."

– Maya Angelou,
Poet Laureate

What one Nothing New aspect could you add to your life? Maybe not for a year but for a month? A day? There are infinity times infinity reasons to say no thank you to a challenge like this. I have heard many:

"I could never do it."
"I don't have the time, energy, discipline."
"I love shoes too much – like they are my children."
"I would never be able to convince my roommate, wife, husband, partner, roommate to buy into it."

Decide and commit! You would end up putting your own boundaries on what the time period would look like for trying your own Nothing New experiment. You would set up your own rules with some level of discomfort or effort required, otherwise what's the point? AND some boundaries, as in, "I am not going to live outside for a year, weave fabric for clothing or make my own soap." Should you take on a challenge like this, you will most likely set up your own stipulations. Again, it is my opinion there needs to be some level of pain for there to be a noteworthy change AND within reason in your own lifestyle to be able to sustain your changes…

Former Navy SEAL commander, Rhodes Scholar, Eric Greitens, Ph.D says it all in an Outside Magazine interview about commitment:

"It's all about energy. Whether you're leading a nonprofit organization, running a private company, doing something outdoors, or conducting military operations – you have to build habits that keep your energy high. This is my formula: (1) Vigorous exercise: Six days a week, I walk out of a gym, a dojo, or off a track pouring with sweat. (2) Good fuel: When I eat clean, quality food during the day, my energy never sags. (3) Good partners: Working with a team of positive people keeps your spirits up. (4) Balance: I pray every day, and I also laugh, a lot. You won't have focus without balance. (5) A goal: A worthy challenge will take care of your motivation for you."

You Can Do It – Ten Easy Steps

1. Know your why – your Nothing New purpose will guide all your actions.
2. List your hot spots – stores, certain items, experiences you want to avoid (says the Cardigan Queen).
3. Set your timeframe for a day, month, year – all are valid, be proud!
4. Engage your people – whoever stands to benefit or be affected by your Nothing New.
5. Keep a journal or blog about your experience – there WILL be things you'll want to remember.
6. Track your spending in some way – in a notebook, folder or online.
7. Involve key supporters to listen to your stories and help you make good decisions.

8. Focus on the changes you are making not on the changes you want others to make.
9. Hold yourself accountable and understand how to get back on track when you slip.
10. Tell your story...

That is all. Oh and keep us posted! Share your successes, ideas and resources on the Teamworks website: *www.betterteams.com.*

Epilogue
YEAR TWO AND BEYOND

"It comes from saying no to 1,000 things to make sure we don't get on the wrong track or try to do too much."

**– Steve Jobs,
Computer engineer (1955-2011)**

I took two months off after my Year of Nothing New before starting Year Two on May 18, 2011. I sort of hung out and allowed myself to buy a few new things before "going back" to Nothing New. I felt a little bit like I was coming out of the wilderness to obtain provisions before going back into the woods. Quite a different wilderness in Fairport, NY compared to perhaps a Walden Pond or Antarctic trek – an adventure, nonetheless.

Year Two Challenges

Year Two was a little different. In addition to not buying new again for the year, I added 6 more Motivations and continued on with a few select good habits.

1. No TV
I took the TV out of my living room which made it was easy to NOT watch. It was a little more challenging at a friend's house or in a hotel room. I didn't watch any TV on

the web either. The cable dude said "Wow, good luck with that" when I told him what I was doing as he cancelled my service. This saved me $96 a year! I reduced my landline plan by $240 a year on the same call for a total savings of $336. (PS. I have since cancelled my landline and my fax number and saved $480 a year). After a month of no TV, I stopped missing it. I got out of the habit of watching altogether and of having it on in the background as company. I had no idea of what was happening on *The Bachelorette*, so my life felt more peaceful, my mind less cluttered and my travel less stressful. I did not miss hearing all the bad news, the over-amplified commercials or the re-re-re-runs. I read two non-work related books, got more work done, wrote postcards on vacation, talked with my family and friends more and took care of other miscellany like follow-up emails, logging receipts, and balancing my checkbook during the light of day. I was more organized and got things done along the way instead of letting them pile up – AND in order of importance (yes), on time (monumental feat) and with less stress (for real).

2. No Chain Coffee Shops

I had gotten into a bad habit of enjoying a frequent, iced grande caramel macchiato. I was using it to celebrate everything from a successful workshop, to working with a new client, to "Today is Tuesday"...not good. I shouldn't have even been drinking coffee or milk! I have a sensitivity to coffee plus lactose intolerance – never mind it is $4 every time. Imagine a year of savings, $4 x 52 = $208. An easy solution to bring my own tea and reusable mug when I met someone at a coffee shop. I had three fails in my NN Year 2. I have no justification.

3. Transportation
Maintained my two no-drive days a week in Year Two and up to the present.

4. Lights
I maintained a one light rule in the hotel. Along with no TV in Year 2, I got more sleep and more work done. This habit is a lasting one.

5. Trash
Brought all my trash home from traveling for Year 2 and I was fully aware of how much garbage I was creating out there. Now I bring all the recyclables if the hotel, camp or retreat center doesn't recycle.

6. Handmade Gifts
Year 2 was candle-holders, Year 3 was lavender scrub again and Year 4 (2013) is going to be Peppermint Bark. And of course, always Skarie's Spicy Walnuts.

I Can See Garlic from My House

I planted again in Year 2 and became an expert at killing zucchini and beets…again. Doubled the size of the garden in Year 3 to maximize the same space as a 14 x 14 garden. Turned the raised beds 90 degrees for better sun and rented a tiller from Home Depot to turn over all the grass. A lot of work and I was glad to have more space. Did buy new wood and brackets and repurposed a few found items in my garage – fence posts and wire. Bought used tiles from the Habitat Restore to mark the path between the beds. New seeds. Became even more of a weather app geek; My Radar, NOAA and The Weather Channel. I planted some of F&L's garlic in 2011 and then it happened. I glanced out my kitchen window one May Sunday to scan for branches, squirrels and cardinals and realized I could see the garlic sprouts! I could really see them...8 of the 12 garlic cloves I planted in November sprouting up about an inch above the soil. And the Gardener was happy. Their garlic – now my garlic – was second generation. I have since grown garlic twice more and have harvested my own third generation in 2013. Proud Mama.

"To remove the garlic from the ground, take a flat shovel and gently loosen the dirt around them. Lift the bulbs out gently. Garlic can bruise easily and bruised garlic does not keep. Don't bump it, don't bounce it. Don't drop it." – Garlic

It really is a life metaphor to see something survive and thrive through what seemed like the longest, coldest, grayest winter EVER. Plant something, let it sit and see it sprout. Life. As I planted kale, tomatoes, butternut squash, more basil and more lettuce in Year 2, I was seeing how this whole grow-your-own thing could become a way of life. Don't worry, I will not be going out to obtain chickens and goats at this point. I will leave the animal rearing to the experts and bow down to all farmers and animal tenders for the time, energy and patience it must take to raise animals. I mean really, Buddy and Curtis require some tending, but they are pretty self-sufficient. There, I did it – a way to mention my cats by name in this book.

Swimming

Got back in the pool and it has changed me for good.

Spending

I tracked my two months off of spending and report accordingly here – total was $338. Then I went back Year 2 of Nothing New.

$5   2 shower curtains
$26   To-Go Ware Set (one for Gina and one for me)
$307   Conference clothing for 2011 and 2012, shoes, boots – all from my favorite mall store and Anything Goes consignment store…wait, let me explain! I got rid of all the items I never wore and what I had left did not fit…

Teamworks

With more time to dream and plan, I created a new program called Lead Green, did a successful fundraiser at a conference for Dress for Success, revived an internship program and redefined my customer service philosophy:

- Transparency
- Integrity
- Partnership
- Collaboration
- The right match
- Personal touch

Nothing New Fund

Anytime I bought something new or outside my boundaries, I put the dollar amount into a separate account to be donated at the end of the year. In addition, if there was an item I really wanted, or almost bought because I would have under any other circumstances, that amount went in too.

$11   Coveted San Francisco mug
$40   Desired 40 piece set of second hand red plates/cups/
        bowls – did not need, did not buy
$9   Coffee while traveling in plastic cup
$16   Meals on plane in plastic container
$20   Boat hardware
$70   Wood and brackets
$2   Bamboo stakes
$97   2 Ugly Dolls (for my nephews)
$15   Travel mug (forgot mine on a trip)
$17   7 lavender plants (for gift making later)
$75   Sunglasses (New shades – $75. Learning to not let
        sunglasses fall out of your lap while getting out of the
        car to see the new puppies and letting them fall onto
        the street without noticing and a car running over
        them – Priceless.)
$321 Materials for making presents for 19 people
$64   Paint and supplies for painting bedroom

$757   TOTAL

Bought New – Needed

$300 Printer
$800 Snow tires
$250 Summer tires
$350 Roof shingles for leaking back porch roof
$359 Water heater
$337 Furnace fixed
$52   Plastic for winterizing old windows

$2448 TOTAL

Saved

Put your Judgment-Free Hat on now. Remember, I know about my privilege here.

Item/Area of Expenditure	March 09-10	March 10-11	Difference
Food	$4861	$3862	$999 – Excellent
Clothing	$2767	$282	$2485 – I think I had a problem...
Household	$2038	$387	$1651 – Good
Heat	$1006	$628	$378 – Weather was a factor, still...
Electricity	$428	$373	$55 – More excellent!
Total	**$11,110**	**$5532**	**$5568**

Want List 2013

- Outdoor furniture and fire pit for the backyard
- Cross country ski boots – and new skis if I cannot find the right boots
- Snow shoes
- Light (or ceiling fan) for dining room
- A sauna – what? Maybe someday...
- Better compost system
- Ceiling fan on the front porch (have it just need to install it...)
- Solar panels
- Rain collection barrel

Need List 2013

- New roof
- New porch ceiling
- Paint for the house trim

Note the difference?

Bibliography
LOCAL AND GLOBAL RESOURCES

*"When you plant a tree, never plant only one.
Plant three – one for shade, one for fruit, one for beauty."*

– African proverb

These companies, organizations, and destinations were invaluable to me during this year and have helped me change the way I live, shop and eat…check these out then research your area. Included are some good books, articles, and websites. Have a Nothing New Day – Enjoy!

Rochester, NY – Quality, vision and opportunity – Abundance right in our backyard!

Anything Goes: First-class clothing consignment
Can Kings: In East Rochester – saving the computers, tvs and
    appliances from the landfills!
Craft Bits and Pieces: Never know what you'll find there – benefits
    Fairport/Perinton Senior Living Council
Fairport Farmers' Market: Say hi to Fimka and Larry – organic
    produce, homemade bread and pickled garlic scapes
Lori's Natural Foods: Tons of local, seasonal, organic grooviness

Martinizing Dry Cleaners: Green cleaning process, kind and helpful
Mooseberry Soap Company: Soap, café, indoor market, classes
Nalgene: Yes that Nalgene! Now BPA free reusable water bottles…
Rochester Public Market: Award winning market – took me ten
    years to make it there – don't you wait too long
Rochester Roots: Creating a locally sustainable food system
    ensuring community food security
Towpath Café: Right on the canal in Fairport – good coffee, natural
    light, quiet writing space
Wegman's: Excellent grocery store (MA, MD, NJ, NY, PA, VA) – #5
    Fortune 100 Best Companies 2013

Buy your books used, go to the library or borrow them. This is only a small sample…start here then do your own research…

Food:
Diet for A Small Planet: Francis Moore Lappe
Food Rules: Michael Pollan
Omnivore's Dilemma: Michael Pollan
Cooperative Extensions (Find your extension): www.csrees.usda.gov
Cornell Cooperative Extension (Learn how to grow it):
    www.cce.cornell.edu
Edible Finger Lakes (Local goodness): www.ediblefingerlakes.com
NY Department of Agriculture and Markets (NY food):
    www.agriculture.ny.gov
Pick Your Own (Regional Food – a gem): www.pickyourown.org

De-Clutter:
A Year Without "Made in China": Sara Bongiorni
Give It Up! My Year of Learning to Live Better with Less: Mary
    Carlomagno
Not Buying It: My Year without Shopping: Judith Levine
The 100 Thing Challenge: Dave Bruno
Zen Habits: www.zenhabits.net

Earth Care:
Living Off the Grid: Dave Black
No Impact Man: Colin Beavan
Sufficient: Tom Petherick
Association of University Leaders for a Sustainable Future:
    www.ulsf.org
Decade of Education for Sustainable Development: www.desd.org
Earth Easy: www.eartheasy.com
Greenwashing Index: www.greenwashingindex.com
Lighter Footstep: www.lighterfootstep.com
Sustainable Communities: www.sustainable.org

Health/Home Care:
Aveda (First wind-powered cosmetic company): www.aveda.com
Burt's Bees (Personal care items): www.burtsbees.com
Dr. Bronner's (Magic soap): www.drbronner.com
Made in USA: www.madeinusaforever.com
Organica Jane (Holistic aromatherapy): www.organicajane.com
Preserve Toothbrushes (Recycled yogurt cups):
    www.preserveproducts.com
Recycled Products: www.recycledproducts.com
Seventh Generation (Cleaning products):
    www.seventhgeneration.com
To-Go Ware (Bamboo utensil set): www.to-goware.com
Tom's of Maine (Toothpaste and more): www.tomsofmaine.com

Service/Leadership:
Girl Scouts of the USA (More than cookies): www.girlscouts.org
Greenleaf Center for Servant Leadership (Yes please): www.greenleaf.org
LeaderShape, Inc. (For a just, caring, world): www.leadershape.org
Kiwanis International (Serving children of the world): www.kiwanis.org
Positive Psychology (Focus on the happy): www.pps.sas.upenn.edu

Share/Donate/Give Away:
Change Purse (Anti-human-trafficking efforts):
www.changepurse.org
Clothes4Souls (Small business in developing countries):
www.clothes4souls.org
Dress for Success (Empowering women): www.dressforsuccess.org
Freecycle (Free stuff – want and offer): www.freecycle.org
Mid-Atlantic Clothing Recycling (D.A.R.E. America):
www.mac-recycling.org
Open Door Mission (Homeless in Rochester):
www.opendoormission.com
Share Your Soles (Shoes for kids and adults):
www.shareyoursoles.org
The Fred Rogers Company (Sweaters): www.fredrogers.org
Vietnam Veterans of America (More yes): www.vva.org
Volunteers of America (And YES): www.voa.org
WGirls (Prom dresses): www.wgirls.org

Travel:
Eco Green Hotels: www.ecogreenhotel.com
Green Hotels: www.greenhotels.com
Green Hotel Reviews: www.greenhotelreviews.com

BIBLIOGRAPHY

Allen, W. (2010). *Growing power vision*. Retrieved from http://www. growingpower.org

Bittman, M. (2011). Is junk food really cheaper? *New York Times Sunday Review*. Retrieved from http://www.nytimes. com/2011/09/25/opinion/sunday/is-junk-food-really-cheaper. html?pagewanted=all&_r=0

Carbon Footprint Calculator. (2013). Retrieved from http://www. carbonfootprint.com

Carlin, G. (1986). *Stuff*. Retrieved from http://www.youtube.com/ watch?v=MvgN5gCuLac

Center for Urban Education for Sustainable Agriculture. (2013). Retrieved from http://www.cuesa.org/learn/how-far-does-your-food-travel-get-your-plate

Container Recycling Institute. (2013). *Bottled water*. Retrieved from http://www.container-recycling.org/index.php/issues/bottled-water

Covey, S. (1989). *The seven habits of highly effective people: powerful lessons in personal change*. New York: Fireside/Simon & Schuster.

Duke University Center for Sustainability and Commerce. (2013). *How much do we waste daily?* Retrieved from http://center. sustainability.duke.edu/resources/green-facts-consumers/how-much-do-we-waste-daily

Ellsbury, H. (2011). *Plastic water bottles impose health and environmental risks*. Ban the Bottle. Retrieved from http://www. banthebottle.net/articles/plastic-water-bottles-impose-health-and-environmental-risks/

Federal Aviation Association. (2013.) *Recycling, Reuse and Waste Reduction at Airports*. Retrieved from http://www.faa.gov/ airports/resources/publications/reports/environmental/media/ RecyclingSynthesis2013.pdf

Fershleiser, R. (2008). *Not quite what I was planning*. New York: HarperCollins.

Finley, R. (2013). *A guerilla gardener in south central LA*. Retrieved from http://www.ted.com/talks/ron_finley_a_guerilla_gardener_ in_south_central_la.html

Food and Drug Administration. (2010). *Bottled water everywhere: keeping it safe*. FDA Consumer Health Information. Retrieved from http://www.fda.gov/downloads/forconsumers/consumerupdates/ ucm217437.pdf

Greitens, E. (2010). *Overachieve*. Outside Magazine. Retrieved from http://www.outsideonline.com/outdoor-adventure/politics/9--Overachieve.html

Huffington Post. (2010). Harvard University. *6.7% of world has college degree*. Retrieved from http://www.huffingtonpost. com/2010/05/19/percent-of-world-with-col_n_581807.html

Jagger, M. & Richards, K. (1968). You Can't Always Get What You Want. *On Let It Bleed*. London: Decca (1969). Retrieved from www. metrolyrics.com

Kingsolver, B. (2007). *Animal, vegetable miracle – a year of food life.* New York: HarperCollins.

Leonard, A. (2010). *The story of stuff.* New York: Free Press.

National Geographic. (2013). *Drinking water: Bottled or from the tap?* Retrieved from http://kids.nationalgeographic.com/kids/stories/spacescience/water-bottle-pollution/

National Oceanic and Atmospheric Administration. (2010). *New Report Warns of Expanding Threat of Hypoxia in U. S. Coastal Waters.* Retrieved from http://www.noaanews.noaa.gov/stories2010/20100903_hypoxia.html

National Public Radio. (2013). *One airport's trash is two million worms' treasure.* Retrieved from http://www.npr.org/blogs/thesalt/2012/12/20/167520020/one-airports-trash-is-2-million-worms-treasure

National Resources Defense Council. (2006). Trash landings: Airlines toss enough cans each year to build a fleet of airliners. Retrieved from http://www.nrdc.org/media/pressreleases/061212.asp

National Trust. (2013). National childhood report. Retrieved from http://www.nationaltrust.org.uk

Neal's Yard Remedies. (2013). *Safe cosmetics.* Retrieved from https://us.nyrorganic.com/shop/corp/area/products/

Pollan, M. (2008). *In defense of food: an eater's manifesto.* New York: Penguin Press.

Privilege [Def. 1]. (n.). *Merriam-Webster Online*. In Merriam-Webster. Retrieved from http://www.merriam-webster.com/dictionary/privilege.

Rochester Roots. (2007). *Mission*. Retrieved from http://www.rochesterroots.org

Rooney Doland, E. (2013). *Unitasker Wednesday: Egg and Spoon Race*. Retrieved from http://unclutterer.com/2013/06/05/unitasker-wednesday-egg-and-spoon-race/

Schwartz, A. (2011). *Sunchips silence its ear-splitting bio-bag*. Fast Company. Retrieved from http://www.fastcompany.com/1731385/sunchips-silences-its-earsplitting-bio-bag

Schwartz, J. (2009). *Buying local: how it boosts the economy*. Time Business and Money. Retrieved from http://content.time.com/time/business/article/0,8599,1903632,00.htmlTime Magazine

St. Vincent Millay, Edna. "First Fig". *A Few Figs From Thistles: Poems and Four Sonnets*. New York: Frank Shay. 1921. 9. Print.

The Good Human. (2007). *Naturally unclog a drain with vinegar, baking soda and water*. Retrieved from http://thegoodhuman.com/2007/03/21/naturally-unclog-drain-with-vinegar/

Thomas, W. (2009). Tighten your food budget and count the savings. *Lessons Learned from the Flock*. (2009). Retrieved from http://simplethrift.wordpress.com/2009/04/21/tighten-your-food-budget-and-count-the-savings/

US Census Bureau, (October 2012). *The big payoff: educational attainment and synthetic estimates of work-life earnings*. Retrieved from http://www.census.gov/prod/2012pubs/acsbr11-04.pdf

Wilson, E. (2010). *Shoppers on a "diet" tame the urge to buy*. New York Times Style Magazine. Retrieved from http://www.nytimes.com/2010/07/22/fashion/22SIXERS.html?pagewanted=all&_r=0

Gratitudes

MANGE TUSEN TAKK
(MANY THOUSAND THANK YOU'S)

"Go in peace. Live justly. Walk humbly with the earth. Love life."

– Reverend Kenneth A. Childs,
Campus minister/advocate (1942-1998)

John Skarie – for late night kitchen talks and teaching me to answer Yes to "Did you learn anything?" – I miss you every day.

Marcia Skarie – for being the Best Mother Ever and answering every one of my calls with "Oh hi honey", then listening with unconditional love to my stories, struggles and wins.

Erik Skarie – for challenging me to consider all sides of an issue and for our shared, unusual sense of humor.

Glenda Skarie – Mi hermanita – for letting me talk with Jonathan and Alexander about toothbrushes made from yogurt cups.

Sue Mahon – for 24 hour a day support and hilarious British comedy YouTube clips.

Nancy Hunter Denney – for the initial supportive response on Day 1 and 1000% reinforcement in the final days writing.

Wendy Fraser – My "sistah" – for her wisdom and grace, our weekly check-ins and her book *Love I.V.*

Pat McCabe – for her enthusiastic support for Nothing New and always being the voice of reason at the kitchen table.

Claudia Blumenstock – for her consistent, non-judgmental inquiry, "How's the writing going?"

Hannah Galan and Lori Galan – for their trusting friendship and care for my cats allowing me travel peace of mind.

Joe O'Gorman – for knowing someday I would understand the value of frugal living and getting three estimates.

Michaela Brew and Vicki Brew – for never doubting me and marveling at my handmade gifts.

Don Crittenden – for setting the bar high with Second Best Bed Publications, I am K in your book.

Shelby Radcliffe – for giving me access to her library and her very welcome "unsolicited advice."

Teri Scanlon – for the original inspiration and your joie de vivre.

Kelsey Wong – for her creativity, energy and brilliant ideas to change the world one Clothing Swap at a time.

Christina Bakos and David Dodge – for their mentorship, friendship and Leading Green with Teamworks.

Fimka and Larry Cooley – for your Faith like a mustard seed and for your precious garlic.

Amy Jane Stewart (Organica Jane) – for the initial detox guidance and resources.

John Roever – for your innovative teaching and for inspiration in my final days of writing with your caring words from 1979.

LeaderShape, Inc. – for the vision process and the tools for living in possibility to create a "just, caring, thriving world where everyone leads with integrity and has a healthy disregard for the impossible."

Kiwanis Club of Brighton – for being a catalyst for my "service renaissance" and giving me the chance to deliberately volunteer at Henry Hudson School #28 in Rochester, NY.

Friends of Teamworks – for your trust in me and sharing your encouraging stories of how spending, shopping, working and living with purpose has impacted your life and the world around you.

Monica Guilian – for beautiful design work and joyfully fixing the "8th blade of grass from the left."

Dan Seseske – for speedy, accurate, kind editing in a world of slow moving critics.

Josh Visser – for fitting this in, making it work and for your role in world peace.

Ryan T. Collier – for the fun photo shoot on the hottest day of the year.

Sandy Gould – for peaceful gardening conversations and calm, expert printing advice.

Virginia Chiccino and Rhonda Miles, Anything Goes Clothing – for your unbridled enthusiasm for A Year of Nothing New.

Mary Bartolotta, Mooseberry Soap Company – for helping me simplify my routine…soap is enough.

Todd Sankes, Martinizing Dry Cleaners – for your positivity and your commitment to green business practices.

My Neighbor's Tree
DAY 265 of Year 2 – February 6, 2012 – Monday

(NOTE: A bit of a side departure from Nothing New – I hope you feel how this relates to being deliberate in the use of all our resources. Thank you for reading.)

They are cutting down my neighbor's tree. I noticed a space in the sky when I pulled down our street on Saturday night – I had been only been gone for the day and something felt different. Then I saw it. A big orange spray painted "X" on the tree two houses up the street from mine. A few of the bigger limbs and branches had already been trimmed. I knew what it meant. It crossed my mind how a green X would have been better – a little more natural, more gentle. I forgot to look again on Sunday in the light of day. The pending demise of this important tree went out of my thoughts as I focused on my travel recovery and everything I had to finish this week. A denial tactic no doubt to avoid thinking about the fate of this tree. When I heard the trucks this morning, I remembered...

Dear Neighbor's Tree,

We were not close friends yet I felt your welcome to Monroe Street every time I returned home. Heading down my street – our street – was the last segment of all of my journeys, from daily errands or from a week away. The GPS would say, "turn right," then "you have reached your destination," as I rounded the corner. There you stood. Your tall reach was an entry way to our little neighborhood. I always appreciated you...I never took the time to really get to know you. I am not even sure what type of tree you are – maybe it doesn't matter. Maybe it's wasn't my place to get to know you – you were not MY tree. Maybe your owners knew you better – I hope so. You sat right in their front yard only a few feet from their house. You offered your shade in the summer, your leaves in the fall, your beacon of green in the spring and your steady presence through the winter. As I witness your last day – a rare, sunny, blue sky day – all your branches are gone now – sections of your trunk hit the lawn with a thud a chunk at a time. I am sad for you and for us. Maybe this is the inevitable return to your roots. Oh Neighbor's Tree, I promise to treasure your cousins – the six black walnut trees marking the corner of my backyard and the white pine tree gracing my front yard. I promise to notice your other relatives more and to remember how many of you were here long before we were and will be here long after we are gone. Thank you for your years of service to Monroe Street, for befriending the apple trees you have seen come and go in this former orchard and for your peaceful reminder…everything is temporary…even the good things…and today is enough.

Love,

Your Neighbor – Kristin Skarie

"In our every deliberation we must consider the impact of our decisions on the next seven generations."

**– Great Law of Peace of the Haudenosaunee,
The Constitution of the Iroquois Nations, 1090**

About the Author

Kristin Skarie is President of Teamworks, a national team building and leadership development consulting company. She is a speaker, educator and entrepreneur with 29 years of experience in higher education administration, organization development and small business advancement. Her background in student affairs includes residence life, student activities, orientation and leadership development in the US, the UK, Malaysia and South Africa. In addition to working with hundreds of universities, hospitals, and companies, she is a Co-Lead Facilitator for the LeaderShape Institute, a Trainer for the National Coalition Building Institute and Vice President of the American College Personnel Association Foundation. She is a grateful recipient of several recognitions including Diamond Honoree (ACPA), Distinguished Alumna (Indiana University), Outstanding Service to the Association (College Student Personnel Association of NY) and Administrator Excellence (Springfield College). Kristin is a Pencil Partner Volunteer with the Rochester City School District, and a gardener, swimmer and sailor. She received her Bachelor's of Science in Physical Education from the University of Wisconsin and her Master's of Science in Education in Higher Education and Student Affairs from Indiana University.

More from Kristin Skarie

Sustainable Leadership: Engaging Students to Create Lasting Change on Campus, IUSPA 2013 Journal
Wisdom Along the Way – Writings on Life and Leadership
Nothing New Blog – www.mostlynothingnew.blogspot.com
Lessons from the Road – Inspirational Insights from Leading Speakers in Education

Book Ordering Information

For additional copies of "A Year of Nothing New – Tools for Living Lean and Green," or to inquire about how to order discounted quantities for your association meetings, leadership conferences, classes, professional staff development, bookstores and gift list, contact the publisher directly at:

Nothing New Publishing
2604 Elmwood Avenue, #246
Rochester, NY 14618
585.330.9181
www.betterteams.com

Have a New Nothing Day!